# CDs, Super Glue, and Salsa

## HOW EVERYDAY PRODUCTS ARE MADE

# CDs,
## Super Glue,
## and Salsa

### HOW EVERYDAY PRODUCTS ARE MADE

## Volume 2
### L - Z

*An imprint of Gale Research Inc.,*
*an International Thomson Publishing Company*

I(T)P

NEW YORK • LONDON • BONN • BOSTON • DETROIT • MADRID
MELBOURNE • MEXICO CITY • PARIS • SINGAPORE • TOKYO
TORONTO • WASHINGTON • ALBANY NY • BELMONT CA • CINCINNATI OH

*CD's, Super Glue, and Salsa: How Everyday Products Are Made*
Sharon Rose and Neil Schlager

**Staff**
Kathleen L. Witman, U•X•L Assistant Developmental Editor
Carol DeKane Nagel, U•X•L Developmental Editor
Thomas L. Romig, U•X•L Publisher

Margaret A. Chamberlain, Permissions Specialist (Pictures)

Catherine Kemp, Production Assistant
Evi Seoud, Assistant Production Manager
Mary Beth Trimper, Production Director

Mark Howell, Page and Cover Designer
Cynthia Baldwin, Art Director

The Graphix Group, Typesetting

Library of Congress Cataloging-in-Publication Data
CD's, super glue, and salsa : how everyday products are made / edited by Sharon Rose.
       p.  cm.
Includes bibliographical references and indexes.
Contents: v. 1. A-K — v. 2. L-Z
ISBN 0-8103-9791-9 (set). — ISBN 0-8103-9792-7 (v. 1). —ISBN 0-8103-9793-5 (v. 2).
1. Manufactures—Juvenile literature.  [1. Manufactures.]
I. Rose, Sharon.
TS146.C37  1995
670—dc20                                                                94-35243
                                                                           CIP
                                                                            AC

This book is printed on acid-free paper that meets the minimum requirements of American National Standard for information Sciences—Permanence Paper for Printed Library Materials, ANSI Z39.48-1984.

Printed in the United States of America

I(T)P™ U·X·L is an imprint of Gale Research Inc.,
          an International Thomson Publishing Company.
          ITP logo is a trademark under license.                    10 9 8 7 6 5 4 3 2

# Contents

# Reader's Guide

*CD's, Super Glue, and Salsa: How Everyday Products Are Made* is written for a generation born into a fast-moving world of sophisticated electronics and space-age technology. So many common products used at home or in school are complex, automated, push-button, instant access, computerized, microwaved wonders. Simple, streamlined outward appearances disguise the difficult steps taken to imagine, invent, create, and manufacture them.

*CD's, Super Glue, and Salsa* reveals the mysteries behind popular foods and comfortable clothes, complex machinery and creative conveniences. The items selected represent progress and fashion trends that influence industry, transportation, music, diet, entertainment, and lifestyle. Detailed, step-by-step descriptions of processes, simple explanations of technical terms and concepts, and helpful illustrations and photographs highlight each entry.

## Format

The 30 entries in *CD's, Super Glue, and Salsa* are arranged alphabetically in two volumes. Although the focus of each entry is the manufacturing process, a wealth of related information is provided: who invented the product or how it has developed, how it works, from what materials it is made, how it is designed, quality control procedures, future applications, and a list of books and periodicals on where to find more information.

To make it easier to locate areas of interest, the entries are broken up into several sections. Most entries include sections devoted to information about the following:

- Background—history or development
- Raw materials needed for production
- Design of the product—how it works
- Manufacturing process

- Quality control
- Byproducts
- Future products
- Where to learn more

## Additonal Features

Boxed sections and call-outs provide related or special interest facts about a product or its development. More than 60 illustrations and 100 photos supplement the written information. Each volume also contains a general subject index with important terms, processes, materials, and people.

## Comments and Suggestions

We welcome comments on this work as well as suggestions for other products to be featured in future editions of *CD's, Super Glue, and Salsa* Please write: Editor, *CD's, Super Glue, and Salsa,* U•X•L, 835 Penobscot Bldg., Detroit, Michigan 48226-4094; call toll-free: 1-800-877-4253; or fax: 313-961-6348.

# Photo Credits

Photographs and illustrations appearing in *CDs, Super Glue, and Salsa: How Everyday Products Are Made,* were received from the following sources:

©Alan Oddie/Photo Edit: pp. 1, 27; UPI/Bettmann: pp. 3, 82, 192; The Bettmann Archive: pp. 4, 37, 90, 92; ©Dick Luria 1989/FPG International: p. 5; ©David Young-Wolff/Photo Edit: pp. 12, 91, 165, 191, 194, 195, 247, 248; ©1985 Jan Staller/The Stock Market: p. 13; ©1992 Bill Losh/FPG International: p. 17; ©Tony Freeman/Photo Edit: pp. 20, 21, 67, 74, 152, 161, 169, 179, 181, 184, 200, 201, 219, 220, 229, 230, 238, 239, 265, 273, 279; FPG International: pp. 22, 56; Courtesy Levi Straus and Company: p. 28; ©Art Tilley/FPG International: p. 29; ©Gary Connor/Photo Edit: pp. 36, 263; ©Ulf Sjostedt 1990/FPG International: p. 39; Reuters/Bettmann: pp. 46, 48, 117, 212, 271; Illustration by Daniel D. Feaser: p. 47; Brownie Harris/The Stock Market: p. 50; ©Roy Morsch 1988/The Stock Market: p. 54; ©1989 Connie Hansen/The Stock Market: p. 57; ©1982 Charles Schneider/FPG International: p. 62; ©David Hundley/The Stock Market: p. 63; ©Barry Rosenthal Studio, Inc./FPG International: p. 64; ©1989 Thomas Lindsay/FPG International: p. 65; ©Jeffrey Sylvester/FPG International: pp. 73, 137; ©Tom McCarthy Photos, Model Released 1993/Photo Edit: p. 79; ©Thierry Cariou/The Stock Market: p. 80; ©Pete Saloutos 1994/The Stock Market: p. 81; ©Michael Krasowitz 1993/FPG International: p. 89; ©1985 Paul Ambrose/FPG International: pp. 98, 100; ©1985 Dick Luria/FPG International: p. 99; ©Richard Laird 1989/FPG International: pp. 107, 255, 256; ©Chris Sorensen/The Stock Market: pp. 109, 113; ©1993 Richard Mackson/FPG International: p. 112; ©Phil McCarten/Photo Edit: p. 115; ©1991 Jim McNee/FPG International: p. 116; AP/Wide World Photos: pp. 119, 146, 257; ©1991 Ken Korsh/FPG International: p. 138; ©Myrleen Ferguson Cate/Photo Edit: p. 139; ©1989 Ron Scott/The Stock Market: pp. 145, 148; ©1989 John Gillmore/The Stock Market: pp. 154, 155; Courtesy of Bob Huffman: p. 157; ©Peter Johansky/FPG International: p. 164; Don Mason/The Stock Market: p. 172; ©1985 Michael A. Keller/FPG International: p. 174; ©Roy Morsch/The Stock Market: p. 205; From *Earth-*

# Lawn Mower

## The Cutting Edge

The lawn mower is a marvelous mechanical device that takes the push and pain out of cutting a lawn. Power mowers actually shave the surface of the grass with a rapidly rotating blade or blades.

For centuries, grass was cut by workers who hiked through pastures or fields swinging small, sharp scythes (long curved blade with a long handle). The work was tiring, slow, and mostly ineffective—the scythes worked well only when the grass was wet. The first mechanical grass-cutter was invented in 1830 by Edwin Budding, an English textile (fabric) worker. He developed a mower that was based on a textile machine he used to shear (shave) the fuzz off of new cloth.

Budding's cylindrical mower was attached to a rear roller that propelled it with a chain drive, and it shaved grass with a curved cutting edge attached to the cylinder. He created two sizes, large and small. The large mower had to be pulled by horses, whose hooves were temporarily shod (covered) with rubber boots to prevent them from tearing up the turf. The head gardener at the London Zoo was among the first to purchase this model. Budding advertised the smaller mower as "an amusing, useful, and healthy exerciser for country gentlemen."

Country gentlemen and others were not easily convinced. Mechanical grass cutters were slow to catch on, perhaps because Budding's mower was quite heavy and awkward. Only two lawn mower manufacturers exhibited grass cutting machines at England's Great Exhibition in 1851.

*In addition to cutting grass, lawn mowers can bag, vacuum, rake, chop, mulch, shred, recycle and dethatch a lawn.*

A rotary lawn mower.

## Sports Connection

Several decades later the new machines experienced a sudden surge in popularity. This was partly due to the interest in lawn tennis that arose in England during the late nineteenth century. Around this time, Budding's early designs were improved. Weighing considerably less than the first machines, and based on the side wheel design still used in today's most popular mowers, the refined machines were soon visible in yards of trendsetters throughout England.

The earliest gas-driven lawn mowers were designed in 1897 by the Benz Company of Germany and the Coldwell Lawn Mower Company of

New York. Two years later an English company developed its own model; however, none of these companies mass produced (manufactured in great quantity) their designs. In 1902 the first commercially produced power mower, designed by James Edward Ransome, was manufactured and sold. Although Ransome's mower featured a comfortable passenger seat, most early mowers did not, and even today the most popular models are pushed from behind.

Power mowers are presently available in four basic designs: the rotary mower, the power reel mower, the riding mower, and the tractor. Because the rotary mower is the most common, it is the focus of this entry.

Pushed from behind, rotary mowers feature a single rotating blade enclosed in a case and supported by wheels. As the engine turns, it spins the blade. The blade whirls around 3,000 times per minute, about 19,000 feet (5,800 meters) per minute at the tip of the blade where the cutting actually occurs.

The best rotaries feature a horn of plenty (cornucopia) or wind tunnel shape curving around the front of the body (the housing) and ending at the discharge chute through which the mown grass flies out. Self-propelled models are driven by a chain or belt connected to the engine's drive shaft. Gears usually turn a horizontal axle (supporting shaft) which in turn rotates the wheels. Some models have a big chain- or belt-driven movable unit that rises off and settles down on the wheels.

## Reel or Rotary?

The power reel mower features several blades attached at both ends to drums (cylinders) that are attached to wheels. The engine drive shaft that spins the reel can also be rigged to propel (move, push) the mower if the worker wants to save physical energy. Overlapping the grass, this machine's five to seven straight blades pull it against a cutting bar at the bottom of the mower. Then one or more rollers smooth and compact the clippings as the mower goes over them.

Reel mowers are actually more efficient than rotary mowers because the rotaries use only the end of the blade to do most of the cutting, while the fixed blades in a reel mower cut with the entire length of both edges. However, rotary mowers are easier to manufacture because the basic design is simpler, and they work well on almost all lawn types. Most of the 40 million mowers in use on any given summer Saturday are rotary mowers.

Old-fashioned, people-powered, push-type (or hand) lawn mowers still have a market. Every few years these reel mowers enjoy a revival for varying reasons. Promoters point out that they are environmentally correct—cutting down on air and noise pollution as well as grass. Fitness buffs report that they can burn 450 calories per hour while pushing a reel mower around the yard. This makes cutting the grass as aerobically useful as a game of tennis, but probably not quite as much fun.

## Mower Materials

The typical gas-powered walk-behind mower may have as many as 270 individual parts, including a technologically advanced two- or four-cycle engine, a variety of machine made parts, various subassemblies purchased from outside contractors (businesses which specialize in certain parts), and many pieces of standard hardware. Most of these pieces are metal, including the major parts: mower pan, handlebar, engine, and blades. A few, however, are made of plastic, such as side discharge chutes, covers, and plugs.

## The Manufacturing Process

Manufacturing the conventional rotary lawn mower requires precise inventory control (the right amount of all supplies needed), strategic placement of parts and people, and synchronization (working together in unison) of people and tasks. In some instances, robots are used along with trained workers.

### Unloading and distributing the components

1 Trucked into the plant's loading dock, the components (various mower parts) are moved by forklifts or overhead trolleys to other centers for forming, machining, painting, or, if they require no additional work upon arrival, assembly.

### The mower pan

2 The steel mower pan, the largest single part and one used in many models, is first machine-stamped into the proper shape under great heat and pressure. The pan is then transported to a robotic cell, where a plasma cutter cuts openings in it. The term plasma refers to any of a number of gases (argon is commonly used) that can be raised to high temperature and ionized (electrically charged). When directed through the narrow opening of a torch, this hot, ionized gas can be used for both cutting and welding.

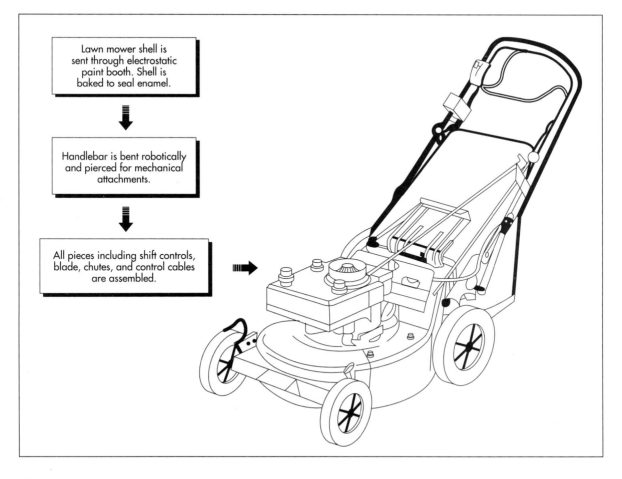

Lawn mower shell is
sent through electrostatic
paint booth. Shell is
baked to seal enamel.

Handlebar is bent robotically
and pierced for mechanical
attachments.

All pieces including shift controls,
blade, chutes, and control cables
are assembled.

Fig. 30. A rotary lawn mower.

3 After other elements such as baffles (deflecting plates) are welded on, the finished pan and a number of other exposed parts are powder painted in a sealed room. Powder painting involves thoroughly washing and rinsing the parts with chemicals to seal the surfaces. The parts are then attached to overhead conveyors (moving tracks) and run through a paint booth. Fine paint particles are sprayed from a gun that gives them an electrostatic charge—opposite to the charge given to the part being painted—that causes the paint to stick to the surface of the mower evenly. Next, the parts are baked in ovens to produce a shiny, permanent, enamel-like coating. The pan and other parts are now ready to withstand years of exposure to corrosive grass fluids, and the dirt and debris kicked up in the cutting process.

### Shaping the handlebar

4 The handlebar is created in a robotic cell where mechanical arms perform three operations. In a bender, the tubing is first bent in at least four places. A second press operation flattens the ends, and a third pierces about fourteen round and square holes into the tubing. These holes will hold the starting mechanism, blade and wheel drive control, and the pan attachment. The finished handlebar is sent to a subassembly station, where many of the controls are added.

### Other subassemblies

5 The other major subassemblies are also created at various plant centers using formed, machined, or purchased materials and standard hardware. Parts purchased from outside suppliers include engines built to manufacturer's requirements, tires, shift mechanisms, wiring harnesses (protective covers for wires), and bearings (devices that reduce friction between moving and non-moving parts). Injection-molded plastic parts are purchased for use in side discharge chutes, covers, and plugs. Injection molding is a process in which melted plastic is squirted into a mold and then allowed to cool. As it cools, the plastic assumes the shape of the mold.

6 Assembly teams put the six or more major subassemblies together on a rolling line. The engine is first placed upside down in a frame fixture, and the mower pan is bolted down along with the drive mechanism. Then come the rear axle, brackets, and rods to secure the shift controls. The blade and accompanying clutch wheels and parts are fastened to the engine through the pan opening with preset power wrenches.

After adding hardware and wheels, the unit is flipped upright onto its wheels. The handlebar is attached, and control cables are secured and set. Finally, the mower—each mower—is performance-tested before shipment to dealers.

## Quality Control

Inspectors monitor the manufacturing process throughout the production run, checking fits, seams, durability, and finishes. In particular, the paint operation is scrutinized. Samples of each painted part are regularly pulled off the line for ultrasonic testing, a process that exposes the paint to the same corrosive action of a salt bath to simulate 450 hours of continuous exposure to the natural outdoor environment. Painted parts

Two children pushing a hand (reel) mower.

are also scribed (scratched) and the exposed surface is watched for tell-tale signs of rust. If needed, the paint or cleaning cycles are adjusted to assure high quality and durable finishes.

Final performance testing—the last step in the assembly— guarantees reliability and safety for users. A small quantity of a gas/oil mixture is added to each engine. A technician cranks the engine to check and measure its RPM (revolutions per minute). Drive elements and safety switches are also checked. As required by current Consumer Product Safety Commission regulations, the mower blade, when running, must stop within three seconds after the control handle is released.

## Robots and Sun Mowers

Today's mowers are a talented bunch. In addition to cutting grass they can bag, vacuum, rake, chop, mulch, shred, recycle, and dethatch a lawn. Industry experts predict still more improvements.

The use of high-impact plastics instead of metal for a mower's structural parts will lighten future machines. One design already built by Dow Plastics Company in Michigan condenses 150 parts of a riding mower into one, strong, molded body. This step alone dramatically cuts assembly time. Plastic is also expected to show higher resistance to chemical corrosion, rust, and dents.

Work is in progress on the ultimate convenience—a computer-guided robotic lawn mower. This handy appliance contains sensors that can "see" uncut grass and a computer "brain" that will guide it. An obstacle detector will steer the machine around trees, shrubs, toys, and people. Homeowners can relax on the porch and control the robot-mower with a joystick.

The lawn mower will also benefit from the development of new and more efficient power sources. A recent invention is the solar-powered lawn mower, which uses energy from the sun rather than gasoline as fuel. It needs no tuneups or oil changes, and it operates very quietly. Perhaps its biggest drawback is the small amount of energy its battery can store: only enough for two hours of cutting, which must be followed by three days of charging. However, as batteries with more storage capabilities are developed, the sun will star in lawn care.

## WHERE TO LEARN MORE

Buderi, Robert. "Now, You Can Mow the Lawn from Your Hammock," *Business Week.* May 14, 1990, p. 64.

Davidson, Homer L. *Care and Repair of Lawn and Garden Tools.* TAB Books, 1992.

Macaulay, David. *The Way Things Work.* Houghton Mifflin Company, 1988.

Panati, Charles. *Extraordinary Origins of Everyday Things.* Harper & Row, 1987.

*Visual Dictionary of Everyday Things.* Dorling Kindersley, 1991.

# Light Bulb

## From Flame to Filament

From the earliest periods of history until the beginning of the nineteenth century, fire was humankind's primary source of light. People lived and worked by the firelight from torches, candles, and oil and gas lamps. It was never quite enough. Besides the danger presented by an open flame (especially when used indoors), firelight was too dim and the smoke too toxic for most purposes.

The first attempts at using electric light were made by English chemist Sir Humphry Davy. In 1802 Davy showed that electric currents could heat thin strips of metal to white heat, producing a good light. This was the beginning of incandescent (glowing with intense heat) electric light.

The next major development was the arc light. This was basically two electrodes (solid electric carriers or conductors), usually made of carbon (a nonmetallic element), separated from each other by a short air space. Electric current applied to one of the electrodes flowed to and through the other electrode resulting in an arc of light across the air space. Arc lamps (or light bulbs) were used mainly in outdoor lighting; the race was still on among a large group of scientists to discover a useful source of indoor illumination.

The biggest problem slowing the development of a commercially useful incandescent light was finding suitable glowing elements. Davy found that platinum (a silver-white metal) was the only metal that could produce white heat for any length of time. Carbon was also used, but it oxidized (mixed with oxygen) very quickly in air, causing it to burn out. The

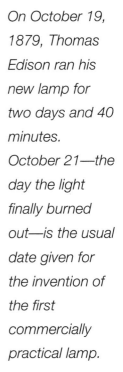

On October 19, 1879, Thomas Edison ran his new lamp for two days and 40 minutes. October 21—the day the light finally burned out—is the usual date given for the invention of the first commercially practical lamp.

Thomas Edison in 1933 holding one of his light bulbs.

solution was to develop a vacuum that would keep air away from the elements, thus preserving the light-producing materials.

Thomas Alva Edison, a young inventor working in Menlo Park, New Jersey, began working on his own form of electric light in the 1870s. In 1877 Edison joined the race to invent a practical electric light source. He started by examining the experiments of others, and finding the reasons for his competitors' failures. In the process, he determined that platinum made a much better burner than carbon. Working with platinum, Edison obtained his first patent (government protection of his invention) in April 1879 on a relatively impractical lamp. Then he continued his search for a material that could be heated efficiently and inexpensively.

Edison also tinkered with other components of the lighting system. He built his own power source and devised a breakthrough wiring system that could handle a number of lamps burning at the same time. His most important discovery, however, was the invention of a suitable filament. This was a very thin, thread-like wire that could hold an electric current without melting or changing. Most of the early filaments burned out very quickly, making these lamps useless for most purposes. To solve this problem, Edison again tried carbon as a means of illumination.

Edison finally selected carbonized cotton thread as his filament material. The filament was clamped to platinum wires that carried an electric current to and from the filament. This assembly was then placed in a glass bulb that was fused at the neck (called sealing-in). A vacuum pump removed the air from the bulb, a slow but important step. Lead-in wires that would be connected to the electrical current stuck out from the base of the glass bulb.

On October 19, 1879, Edison ran his first test of the new lamp. It ran for two days and 40 minutes (October 21—the day the filament finally burned out—is the usual date given for the invention of the first commercially practical lamp). Of course, this original lamp underwent a number of changes and refinements. Manufacturing plants were set up to mass produce light bulbs and great advances were made in wiring and electrical current systems. However, today's incandescent light bulbs greatly resemble Edison's original lamps. The major differences are the use of tungsten (a tough metal with a very high melting point) filaments and various gases for higher efficiency and lumination (brightness) resulting from filaments that can be heated to higher temperatures.

*The average life of the majority of household light bulbs is 750 to 1,000 hours, depending on wattage.*

Although the incandescent lamp was the first and certainly the least expensive type of light bulb, there are now a variety of other light sources that serve many uses:

- Tungsten halogen lamps (have a tungsten filament and are filled with a halogen gas to prolong the filament's life).

- Fluorescent lamps are glass tubes that contain mercury vapor and argon gas. When electricity flows through the tube, it causes the mercury to give off ultraviolet energy. This energy strikes a phosphor coating inside the lamp and makes it glow.

- Mercury vapor lamps have two bulbs—an arc tube (made of quartz) is inside a protective glass bulb. The arc tube contains mercury vapor at a higher pressure than in the fluorescent lamp, allowing the vapor lamp to produce light without using the phosphor coating.

- Neon lamps are glass tubes, filled with neon gas, that glow when an electric discharge takes place in them. The color of the light is determined by the gas mixture; pure neon gas gives off red light.

- Metal halide lamps, used primarily outdoors for stadiums and roadways, contain chemical mixtures of metal and halogen. This type of lamp works in much the same fashion as the mercury vapor lamps except that metal halide can produce a more natural color balance when used without phosphors.

- High-pressure sodium lamps are also similar to mercury vapor lamps; however, the arc tube is made of aluminum oxide instead of quartz, and it contains a solid mixture of sodium and mercury.

## Incandescent Light Materials

This section as well as the manufacturing process will focus on incan-

The most common incandescent lightbulb.

descent light bulbs. As mentioned earlier, many different materials were used for the filament until tungsten became the metal of choice during the early part of the twentieth century. Although extremely fragile, tungsten filaments can withstand temperatures over 4,500 degrees Fahrenheit (2,480 degrees Celsius). The development of the tungsten filament is considered the greatest advancement in light bulb technology because they could be produced cheaply and last longer than any of the earlier materials.

The connecting or lead-in wires are typically made of nickel-iron wire (called dumet because it uses two metals) (see fig. 32). This wire is dipped into a chemical solution to make it stick to glass. The bulb itself is made of

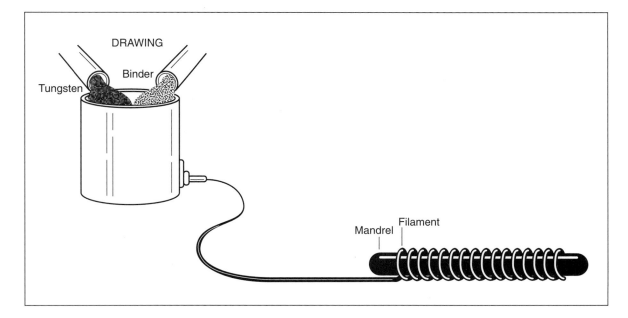

Fig. 31. The filament is one of the main components in a light bulb.

glass and contains a mixture of gases, usually argon and nitrogen, which increase the life of the filament. Air is pumped out of the bulb and replaced with the gases.

A standard-sized base holds the entire assembly in place. The base, known as the "Edison screw base," was originally made of brass and insulated (sealed) with plaster of paris and, later, porcelain (hard ceramic, or china). Today, aluminum is used on the outside and glass is used to insulate the inside of the base, for greater strength.

## The Manufacturing Process

The uses of light bulbs range from street lights to automobile headlights to flashlights. For each use, the individual bulb differs in size and wattage, which determine the amount of light the bulb gives off (lumens). However, all incandescent light bulbs have three basic parts—the filament, the bulb, and the base. Originally made by hand, light bulb manufacture is now almost entirely automated.

### Filament

1 The filament is manufactured through a process known as drawing, in which tungsten is mixed with a binder material and pulled through a die—a shaped opening—into a fine wire (see fig. 31). Next, the wire is wound around a metal bar called a mandrel in order to mold it into its proper coiled shape, and then it is heated in a process known as annealing. This process softens the wire and makes its structure more uniform. The mandrel is then dissolved in acid.

2 The coiled filament is attached to the lead-in wires. The lead-in wires have hooked ends which are either pressed over the end of the filament or, in larger bulbs, spot-welded.

### Glass bulb

3 The glass bulbs or casings are produced using a ribbon machine (see fig. 32). After heating in a furnace, a continuous ribbon of glass moves along a conveyor belt. Precisely aligned air nozzles blow the glass through holes in the conveyor belt into molds, creating the casings. A ribbon machine moving at top speed can produce more than 50,000 bulbs per hour. After the casings are blown, they are cooled and then cut off of the ribbon machine. Next, the inside of the bulb is coated with silica (a fine crystalline mixture) to remove the glare caused by a glowing, uncovered filament. The company emblem and bulb wattage are then stamped onto the outside top of each casing.

### Base

4 The base of the bulb is also constructed using molds. It is made with indentations in the shape of a screw so that it can easily fit into the socket of a light fixture.

### Assembly

5 Once the filament, base, and bulb are made, they are fitted together by machines. First, the filament is mounted to the stem assembly, with its ends clamped to the two lead-in wires. Next, the air inside the bulb is pulled out, and the casing is filled with an argon and nitrogen mixture. These gases ensure a longer life for the filament. The tungsten will eventually evaporate and break. As it evaporates, it leaves a dark deposit on the inside of the bulb known as bulb-wall blackening.

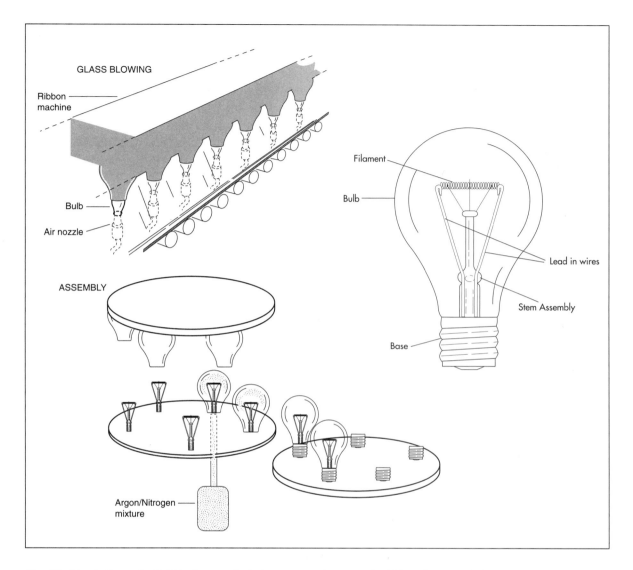

Fig. 32. Nearly the entire light bulb manufacturing process is automated (done by machine). The glass bulbs are blown by a ribbon machine that can produce more than 50,000 bulbs per hour. After the filament and stem assembly are inserted into the bulb, the air inside the bulb is removed and an argon/nitrogen mixture is pumped in.

6 Finally, the base and the bulb are sealed. The base slides onto the end of the glass bulb tightly so that no other material is needed to keep them together. Instead, their matching shapes allow the two pieces to be held together snugly, with the lead-in wires touching the aluminum base to ensure proper electrical contact. After testing, bulbs are placed in their packages and shipped to consumers.

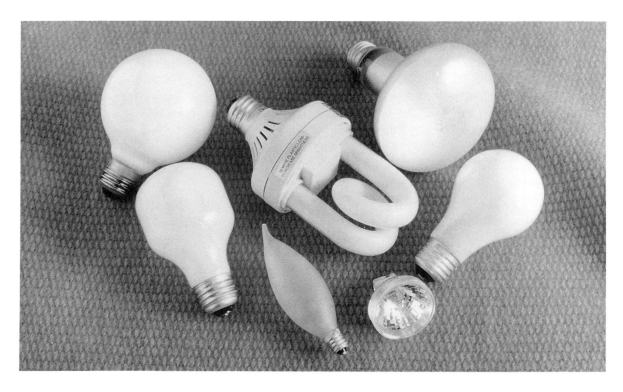

A variety of light bulbs.

## Quality Control

Light bulbs are tested for both lamp life and strength. In order to provide quick results, selected bulbs are screwed into test racks and lit at levels much greater than their normal burning strength. This provides an accurate reading on how long the bulb will last under normal conditions. Testing is performed at all manufacturing plants as well as at some independent testing laboratories. The average life of the majority of household light bulbs is 750 to 1,000 hours, depending on wattage.

## Brighter Ideas

Less than 5 percent of the electric energy used in an incandescent bulb produces light. The remaining 95 percent is converted to heat, and wasted. While heating a filament until it glows is certainly a satisfactory way to produce light, it is extremely inefficient. In a world with dwindling resources, where energy conservation is increasingly important, this inefficiency may eventually make the incandescent light bulb impractical.

There are other light sources already in use that could replace the familiar incandescent bulb. Fluorescent tubes, for instance, already dominate the industrial market, and undoubtedly they will find increasing use as a domestic light source as well. Fluorescent bulbs use at least 75 percent less energy than incandescent bulbs and can last twenty times longer. The recent development of "compact" fluorescent bulbs, which unlike the standard fluorescent tube can screw into a typical household lamp, may expand the domestic market for fluorescent lighting.

Another recent development is the "radio-wave bulb," also called the "E-(for electronic)Lamp." These lights transmit energy from a radio-wave generator to a mercury cloud enclosed in the bulb, which in turn produces ultraviolet light. A phosphor coating on the inside of the bulb then converts the ultraviolet (invisible) light into visible light. Such bulbs use only 25 percent as much energy as incandescents, and they can last a decade or more. Moreover, they are also completely interchangeable with incandescent bulbs.

At present, the only down side to E-Lamps is the price. Radio-wave bulbs will probably cost from $10 to $20 each. However, if they really last for more than 10 years, they're still a bargain. Once these new bulbs hit the market, Edison's bright invention may lose its glow.

## WHERE TO LEARN MORE

Adler, Jerry. "At Last, Another Bright Idea," *Newsweek*. June 15, 1992, p. 67.

"Bright Ideas In Light Bulbs," *Consumer Reports*. October 1992, pp. 664-70.

Coy, Peter. "Light Bulbs to Make America Really Stingy with the Juice," *Business Week*. March 29, 1993, p. 91.

Macaulay, David. *The Way Things Work*. Houghton Mifflin Company, 1988.

Panati, Charles. *Extraordinary Origins of Everyday Things*. Harper & Row, 1987.

Parker, Steve. *Eyewitness Science: Electricity*. Dorling Kindersley, 1992.

# Lipstick

*Lipstick is the least expensive and most popular cosmetic in the world today.*

## Face Paint

People have painted their faces in a quest for beauty or power for many centuries. Cosmetics can be traced back to ancient civilizations. History proves that the use of lip color was common among the Sumerians, Egyptians, Syrians, Babylonians, Persians, and Greeks.

In the sixteenth century, England's Queen Elizabeth I and the ladies of her court colored their lips with red mercuric sulfide—a dangerous habit which no doubt shortened their lives, since the mixture is now known to be poisonous. For years, rouge (a reddish powder) was used to color both the lips and the cheeks, depending on the fashion of the times. Rouge was a safer substitute for mercury—and could also be used as a handy polish for metal and glass.

In Western society during the last half of the nineteenth century, makeup was frowned upon. Painted ladies were either actresses, women with loose morals, or both. Nice girls wouldn't dream of shocking their elders or earning a bad reputation by coloring their faces. They stuck to a fresh-scrubbed natural look.

By the twentieth century, the growth of the film industry and popularity of Hollywood movie stars turned the tide. Modern American women wanted respect, equal rights, and a little glamour. Cosmetics, especially lipstick, were increasingly accepted in polite society.

Improvements in the manufacture of applicators (containers) and metal tubes reduced the cost of cosmetics. This, combined with newfound social acceptance, increased the use and popularity of makeup. By 1915 push up tubes were available, and the first claims of "indelibility" (permanence, long-lasting color) were made.

Lipsticks come in a wide range of colors to coordinate with current fashion trends. Consumers can choose from combinations of pink, purple, red, orange, and brown that are frosted, glossed, or pearlized. In spite of the hype, lipstick is a relatively simple product made of dyes and pigments (powdered coloring material) in a perfumed oil-wax base. Retail prices for lipsticks are relatively low, with good quality products priced at less than $4. More expensive versions are available, with prices ranging up to nearly $50 for designer labels and specialty products. Lip balms (soothing ointments for dried or chapped lips) often sell for less than $1.

More than $1 billion is spent on lipstick each year.

The tubes that hold lipstick range from inexpensive plastic dispensers (holders) for lip balms to highly styled metal for lipsticks. Sizes vary, but generally lipstick is sold in a tube 3 inches (7.6 centimeters) in length and about .50 inch (1.3 centimeters) in diameter. (Lip balms are slightly smaller in both length and diameter.) The tube has two parts, a cover and a base. The base is made up of two pieces, the twisting or sliding of which will push the lipstick up for application. Since the manufacture of the tube involves completely different technologies, we will focus here on the manufacture of lipstick only.

## Lipstick Materials

The primary ingredients found in lipstick are wax, oil, alcohol, and pigment. The wax used usually involves some combination of three types—beeswax, candelilla wax, or the more expensive carnauba (a hard wax from the South American carnauba palm tree). Wax enables the mixture to be formed into the easily recognized lipstick shape. Oils such as mineral, caster, lanolin, or vegetable are added to the wax. Fragrance and pigment are mixed in, as are preservatives and antioxidants (substances that prevent lipstick from spoiling). And while every lipstick contains these ingredients, a wide variety of other enhancers can also be included to make the lipstick smoother, more glossy, or to moisten the lips.

Just as there is no standard to the lipstick size and container shape, there are no standard types of, or proportions for, ingredients used. Beyond the base ingredients (wax, oil, and antioxidants) specialized material amounts vary greatly. The ingredients themselves range from complex organic compounds (mixtures) to entirely natural ingredients. The amounts used determine the characteristics of the lipstick. Selecting lipsticks is, as with all cosmetics, an individual choice, so manufacturers have responded by making a wide variety of lipsticks available to the consumer.

In general, wax and oil make up about 60 percent of the lipstick (by weight), with alcohol and pigment accounting for another 25 percent. A pleasant fragrance is always added, but amounts to one percent or less of the mixture. In addition to using lipstick to color the lips, there are also lip liners, crayons, and pencils. The manufacturing methods described here will focus only on lipstick and lip balms.

## The Manufacturing Process

The manufacturing process boils down to three separate steps: melting and mixing the lipstick; pouring the mixture into the tube; and packaging the product for sale. Since lipstick ingredients can be blended and stored for later use, mixing does not have to happen at the same time as pouring. Once the lipstick is in the tube, packaging for retail sale depends on how and where the product is to be sold.

### Melting and mixing

1 First, the ingredients for the lipstick are melted and mixed separately because of the different types of ingredients used (see fig. 33). One mixture contains the solvents (liquids that can dissolve other ingredients), a second contains the oils, and a third contains the fats and waxy

*Some cosmetic manufacturers are now including sun protection in lipstick production.*

A woman applying lipstick.

materials. These are heated in separate stainless steel or ceramic (fired clay or porcelain) containers.

2 The solvent solution and liquid oils are then blended with the color pigments. The mixture passes through a roller mill, grinding the pigment to avoid a "grainy" feel to the lipstick. This process allows air into the oil and pigment combination, so more mechanical working of the mixture is required to eliminate bubbles. The mixture is stirred for several hours, after which some producers use vacuum equipment to withdraw the air.

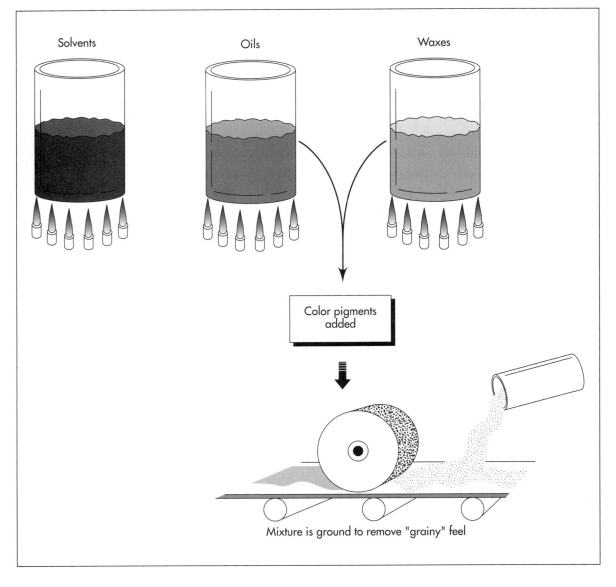

Fig. 33. To make lipstick, the various raw ingredients are first melted separately, then the oils and solvents (dissolving materials) are ground together with the desired color pigments.

3 After the pigment mixture is ground and stirred, it is added to the hot wax until a uniform color and consistency is obtained. The fluid lipstick can then be strained and molded, or it may be poured into pans and stored for future molding.

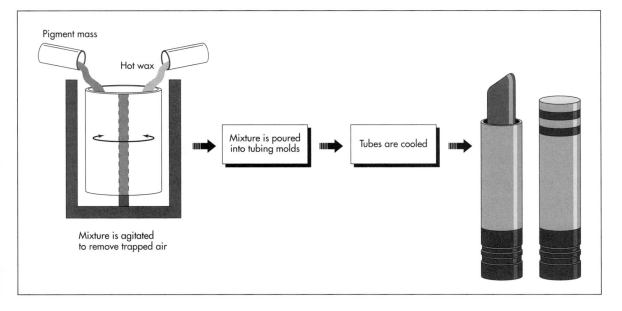

Fig. 34. After the pigment mass is prepared, it is mixed with the hot wax. The mixture is agitated to free it of any air bubbles. Next, it is poured into tubing molds, cooled, and separated from the molds. After final touch-up and visual inspection, the lipstick is ready for packaging.

4 If the fluid lipstick is to be used immediately, the melt is kept at the same temperature, with agitation (constant stirring or quick movement), so that trapped air escapes (see fig. 34). If the lipstick mass is stored, before it is used it must be reheated, checked for color consistency, then maintained at the melt temperature (with agitation) until it can be poured.

Lipsticks are always prepared in batches because of the different color pigments that are used. The size of the batch, and the number of tubes of lipstick produced at one time, will depend on the popularity of the particular shade being made. The amount will determine the manufacturing technique (automated or manual) that is used. Lipstick may be produced in highly automated processes (by machines), at rates of up to 2,400 tubes an hour, or in basically manual operations (by hand or workers), at rates around 150 tubes per hour. The steps in the process differ only in the amounts produced.

## Molding

5 Once the lipstick is mixed and free of air, it is ready to be poured into the tube. A variety of machines are used, and large batches are generally run through a melter that agitates the lipstick mass and

keeps it in liquid form. For smaller, manually run batches, the mass is maintained at the desired mix temperature and agitated in a melter controlled by a worker.

6 The melted mass is poured into a mold, which consists of the bottom part of the metal or plastic tube and a shaping portion that fits snugly with the tube. Lipstick is poured "up-side down" so that the bottom of the tube is at the top of the mold. Any extra is scraped from the mold.

7 The lipstick is cooled (automated molds are kept cold; manually produced molds are transferred to a refrigeration unit). Then the lipstick is separated from the mold, and the bottom of the tube is sealed. Next the lipstick passes through a flaming cabinet (or is flamed by hand) to seal pinholes and improve the finish. The lipstick is visually inspected for air holes, mold separation lines, or marks, and is reworked if necessary.

8 Because lipstick must have a smooth, clean, untouched appearance, rework of the lipstick must be very limited. This explains the importance of the early steps in removing air from the lipstick mass. Lipstick is reworked by hand with a spatula. This can be done in-line, or the tube can be removed from the manufacturing process and reworked.

### Labeling and packaging

9 After the lipstick is retracted (twisted back into the container) and the tube is capped, the lipstick is ready for labeling and packaging. Labels identify the batch and are applied automatically. While there is a great deal of concern about quality and appearance of the finished lipstick product, less attention is given to the appearance of lip balms.

Lip balms are always produced in an automated process (except for experimental or test batches). The heated liquid is poured into the tube in the retracted (closed) position. The tube is then capped by machine—a far less complicated process involving few workers.

10 The final step in the manufacturing process is the packaging of the lipstick tube. There are a variety of packaging options available, ranging from bulk packs which hold more than one lipstick, to individual packs, and including packaging as an item in a make-

A variety of lipstick applicators.

up kit or special promotional offering. Lip balms are packaged in bulk, generally with minimum protection to prevent shipping damage. Packaging for lipsticks varies, and may or may not be highly automated. The package used depends on the where it will be sold rather than on the manufacturing process.

## Environmental Concerns

There is little or no waste in the manufacture of lipstick. Product is reused whenever possible, and since the ingredients are expensive they are seldom thrown out. In the normal manufacturing process there are no by-products, and waste portions of lipstick will be thrown out along with cleaning materials.

## Quality Control

Quality control procedures are strict, since the product must meet government Food and Drug Administration (FDA) standards. Lipstick is the only cosmetic that can be eaten or swallowed, so there are strict controls on ingredients, as well as on manufacturing processes. Lipstick is mixed and processed in a controlled environment so it will be free of contamination (bacteria, germs, or poisons). Incoming material is tested to ensure that it meets regulations. Samples of every batch produced are saved and stored at room temperature for the life of the product (and often beyond that) to maintain a control on the batch.

As noted above, appearance of lipstick as a final product is very important. For this reason everyone involved in the manufacture becomes an inspector, and an imperfect product is either reworked or scrapped. Final inspection of every tube is performed by the customer, and if not satisfactory, will be rejected in the store. Since the retailer (store owner) and manufacturer are usually not the same, quality problems at the consumer level have a major impact on the manufacturer.

Color control of lipstick is critical, so the addition of the pigment is carefully checked when a new batch is manufactured, and the color must be carefully controlled when the lipstick mass is reheated. The color of the mass will change over time, and each time a batch is reheated, the color may be altered. Colorimetric equipment (instruments that measure color by comparison to a chart or amount of pigment) is used to control the shades of lipstick. This equipment gives a numerical reading of the shade when mixed, so it can identically match previous batches. Matching of reheated batches is done visually, so careful time and environmental controls are placed on lipstick mass when it is not immediately used.

## Lipstick Tests

There are two special tests for lipstick: the Heat Test and the Rupture Test.

In the Heat Test, the lipstick is placed in the extended (open) position in a holder and left in an oven with a constant temperature of over 130 degrees Fahrenheit (54 degrees Celsius) for 24 hours. The lipstick should not droop, melt, or change shape.

In the Rupture Test, the lipstick is placed in two holders, in the extended position. Weight is added to the holder on the lipstick portion at 30-second intervals until the lipstick ruptures (bursts). The pressure required to rupture the lipstick is then checked against the manufacturer's standards. Since there are no industry standards for these tests, each manufacturer sets its own stress limits.

## Future Trends

Lipstick is the least expensive and most popular cosmetic in the world today. In 1986 lipstick sales in the United States were more than $720 million. Current estimates put sales at closer to $1 billion per year. There are no accurate figures for current sales of lip balm, since the market is expanding. Manufacturers continue to introduce new types and shades of lipstick, and there is a tremendous variety of product available at moderate cost. As long as cosmetics remain in fashion (and there is no indication that they will not) the market for lipstick will continue to be strong.

## WHERE TO LEARN MORE

Brumber, Elaine. *Save Your Money, Save Your Face.* Facts on File, 1986.

Cobb, Vicki. *The Secret Life of Cosmetics.* Lippincott, 1985.

"New Lipstick Line Cuts Rejects in Half," *Packaging.* August 1992, p. 41.

Panati, Charles. *Extraordinary Origins of Everyday Things.* Harper & Row, 1987.

*Reader's Digest: How in the World?* Reader's Digest, 1990.

# Nail Polish

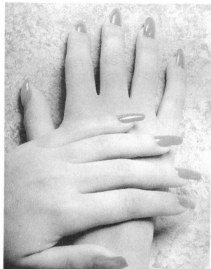

## Painted Nails

Nail polish is a product with more of a future than a past. Unlike many other cosmetics that have a history of hundreds and even thousands of years, nail polish (also called lacquer, or enamel) is a relatively new invention of twentieth-century technology.

Nail coverings were occasionally used in ancient times—the upper classes of ancient Egypt used henna (a reddish-brown dye from the leaves of a henna tree or shrub) to color both hair and fingernails. However, the ingredients of nail polish, its manufacture, and handling are a result of developments in modern chemical technology.

*The main ingredient in nail polish is nitrocellulose cotton, a flammable and explosive material also used to make dynamite.*

Modern nail polish is sold in liquid form in small bottles and is applied with a tiny brush. A few minutes after application, the substance hardens to form a shiny coating on the fingernail that is both water- and chip-resistant. Manufacturers claim that a coating of nail polish should last several days before it begins to chip or peel. When it needs to be removed, nail polish can be neatly erased with nail polish "remover," a fluid designed to break down and dissolve the polish.

## Nail Polish Materials

There is no single formula for nail polish. There are, however, a number of ingredient types that are used. These basic components include: film forming materials, resins (thick, clear, sticky substances found in plants), plasticizers (for keeping the polish soft), solvents (for dissolving other ingredients), and colorings. The exact formula of a nail polish, apart from being a company secret, greatly depends upon choices made by cosmetic company chemists and chemical engineers in the research and development phase of manufacturing. Formulas change as certain ingredients become accepted or rejected for cosmetic use. For example, formaldehyde is a gaseous chemical once used frequently in polish production, but now rarely used because scientists have determined it to be toxic (poisonous).

The primary ingredient in nail polish is nitrocellulose (cellulose nitrate) cotton—a flammable, explosive ingredient also used in making dynamite. Nitrocellulose is a liquid mixed with tiny, near-microscopic cotton fibers. During the manufacturing process, the cotton fibers are ground even smaller and do not need to be removed. The nitrocellulose can be purchased in various consistencies to match the desired thickness of the final product.

A woman carefully polishing her nails.

Nitrocellulose acts as a film-forming ingredient. For nail polish to work properly, a hard film must form on the surface of the nail, but not so quickly that it prevents the material underneath from drying. (Consider commercial puddings or gelatin products that dry or harden on the top surface to protect the moist product underneath.)

Used by itself or with other ingredients, the nitrocellulose film is brittle and does not stick well to nails. Manufacturers add synthetic (manmade) resins and plasticizers (and occasionally similar, natural products) to improve flexibility, and resistance to soap and water. Older recipes sometimes used nylon for this purpose.

Good nail polish should be chip-proof during everyday wear, yet come off easily when remover is applied. However, there is no single resin or

*The "pearl" or "guanine" in pearl nail polish is actually made from small fish scales and skin, suitably cleaned, and mixed with solvents such as castor oil and butyl acetate.*

combination of resins that meets every requirement. Among the resins and plasticizers in use today are castor oil, amyl and butyl stearate, as well as mixes of glycerol, fatty acids, and acetic acids.

The colorings and other ingredients of nail polish must be contained within one or more solvents until the polish is applied. After application, the solvent must be able to evaporate. In many cases, the solvent also acts a plasticizer to keep the product soft. Butyl stearate and acetate compounds are perhaps the most common.

Finally, color is added. Early polishes used easily dissolved dyes, but today's product contains pigments (dry, powdery coloring matter) of one type or another. Choice of pigment and its ability to mix well with the solvent and other ingredients is essential to producing a good quality polish.

Nail polish is a "suspension" product, in which particles (tiny pieces) of color are "suspended" in the solvent for a relatively short period of time, rarely more than two or three years. Shaking a bottle of nail polish before use helps to restore settled particles to the suspension. A very old bottle of nail polish may have so much settled pigment that it is impossible to mix again with the solvent. The problem of settling is perhaps the most difficult one of the manufacturing process.

In addition to coloring pigments, other ingredients can be added to make "frosted," or "pearlized" shades. Micas (tiny reflective minerals), also used in lipsticks, are commonly added, as is "pearl" or "fish scale" material. "Pearl" or "guanine" is actually made from small fish scales and skin, suitably cleaned, and mixed with solvents such as castor oil and butyl acetate. The guanine can also be mixed with gold, silver, and bronze tones.

Pigment choices are restricted by the federal Food and Drug Administration (FDA), which maintains lists of pigments considered acceptable and others that are too dangerous to be used. Manufacturing plants are inspected regularly, and manufacturers must be able to prove they are using only FDA approved pigments. Since the FDA lists of acceptable and unacceptable pigments change with new findings and reexaminations of colors, manufacturers occasionally have to develop a new formula for a popular polish.

## The Manufacturing Process

Early methods of making nail polish used a variety of methods that

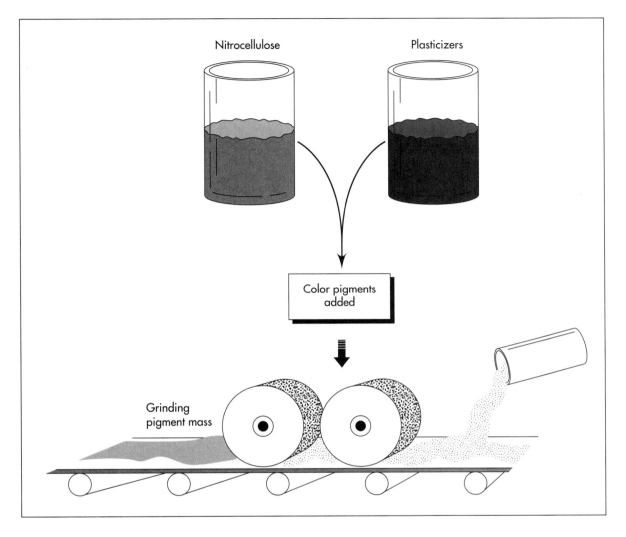

Fig. 35. Nail polish is made by combining nitrocellulose and plasticizers with color pigments. The mixing is done in a "two-roll" differential speed mill, which grinds the pigment between a pair of rollers that work with increasing speed as the pigment is ground down. The goal is to produce a fine dispersion (mix) of the color.

seem strange today. One common technique mixed cleaned scraps of movie film with alcohol and castor oil. The mixture was soaked overnight in a covered container, then strained, colored, and perfumed. Though recognizable as nail polish, the product was far from the high-performance mixtures available today.

Modern nail polish is manufactured in a very sophisticated process using highly skilled workers, advanced machinery, and even robotics.

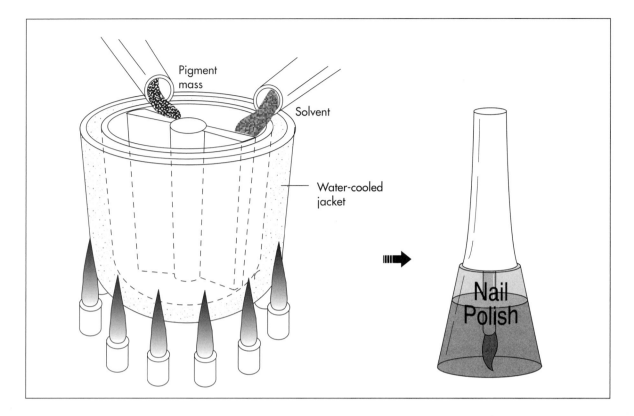

Fig. 36. Once the pigment mass is prepared, it is mixed with solvent in a stainless steel kettle. The kettle has a water-jacket lining to more efficiently cool the mixture.

Today's customers expect a polish to apply smoothly, evenly, and easily; to set relatively quickly; and to be resistant to chipping and peeling. In addition, the polish should not be harmful to surrounding skin.

### Mixing the pigment with nitrocellulose and plasticizer

1 The pigments are mixed with nitrocellulose and plasticizer using a "two-roll" differential speed mill (see fig. 35). This mill grinds the pigment between a pair of rollers that work with increasing speed as the pigment is ground down. The goal is to produce a fine dispersion (spread and mix) of the color.

2 When properly and fully milled, the mixture is removed from the mill in sheet form and then broken up into small chips for mixing with the solvent (see fig. 36). The mixing is performed in stainless

As with most cosmetics, packaging is as important as the product.

steel kettles that can hold anywhere from as little as 5 to as many as 2,000 gallons. Stainless steel must be used because the nitrocellulose is extremely explosive and reacts strongly to the presence of iron. The kettles are jacketed (suspended inside a slightly larger kettle) so that the mixture can be cooled with circulating cold water or another liquid around the outside of the inner kettle. The temperature of the kettle and the rate of cooling are controlled by both computers and technical workers.

This step is performed in a special area designed to control the hazards of fire and explosion. Most modern factories have an area with walls that close in if an alarm sounds and, in case of explosion, with ceilings that safely blow off without endangering the rest of the building.

## Adding other ingredients

3 Materials are mixed in computerized, closed kettles. At the end of the process, the mix is cooled slightly before the addition of other materials such as perfumes and moisturizers.

4 The mixture is then pumped into smaller, 55-gallon containers, and sent by truck to a production line. The finished nail polish is emptied into explosion-proof pumps, and then into smaller bottles suitable for customer use, markets, and store shelves.

## Quality Control

Extreme attention to quality control is essential throughout the manufacturing process. Not only does quality control increase safety in the process, but it is the only way that a manufacturer can earn a customer's confidence and loyalty. A single bottle of poor quality polish can lose a disappointed customer forever. Regardless of quality control, however, no single nail polish is perfect; the cosmetic is always a chemical compromise between what is desired and what the manufacturer is able to produce.

Nail polish is tested throughout the manufacturing process for several important factors (drying time, smoothness of flow, gloss, hardness, color, scratch resistance, etc.). Subjective testing, where the mixture or final product is examined or applied, takes place constantly. Objective laboratory testing of samples, though more time consuming, is also necessary to ensure a usable product. Though laboratory tests are both complicated and unforgiving (no excuses are accepted for flaws), no manufacturer would do without them.

## Future Polish

Perhaps the major problem with nail polishes—from the consumer's point of view—is the length of drying time. Improved fast-drying polishes and quick-dry coatings are showing up on store shelves. Other methods are still being developed, and may result in marketable products.

Of all the different types of cosmetics, nail polish is the one that is most likely to benefit from advancements and developments in the field of chemistry. Chemists will continue to work on polishes, especially since people are paying more attention to their hands and nails. Working women, in particular, consider manicured nails as important to a well-groomed, professional look as neat hair and makeup. The nail polish and manicure industry is going strong and growing.

### WHERE TO LEARN MORE

Balsam, M.S., ed. *Cosmetics: Science and Technology.* Krieger Publishing, 1991.

Boyer, Pamela. "Soft Hands, Strong Nails," *Prevention*. February 1992, pp. 110-16.

*Chemistry of Soap, Detergents, and Cosmetics*. Flinn Scientific, 1989.

Cobb, Vicki. *The Secret Life of Cosmetics*. Lippincott, 1985.

Panati, Charles. *Extraordinary Origins of Everyday Things*. Harper & Row, 1987.

# Optical Fiber

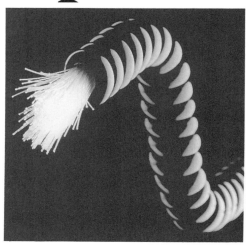

## Through the Glass

Glass is fast replacing metal in the telecommunication industry. Scientists have found that very fine glass fibers can carry messages faster, take up much less space, and won't tolerate any interference or static from other electrical appliances.

An optical fiber is a single, hair-fine filament (thread) drawn from molten silica glass (glass made from melted sand, flint or quartz). These fibers are replacing metal wire as transmitters in high-speed, high-capacity communications systems that change information into light pulses, which is then transmitted along fiber optic cable. Currently, American telephone companies are the largest users of fiber optic cables, but the technology is also used for power lines, some local access computer networks, video transmission, and even medical examinations.

*One of the most remarkable characteristics of optical fiber is that it can hold a strong signal and carry it for a long distance without allowing it to weaken.*

Alexander Graham Bell, the American inventor best known for developing the telephone, first attempted to communicate by using light around 1880. However, light wave communication did not become possible until the mid-twentieth century, when advanced technology provided a transmission source, the laser (a narrow, bright beam of light), and an efficient medium, the optical fiber. The laser was invented in 1960 and, six years later, researchers in England discovered that silica glass fibers would carry light waves without significant attenuation, or loss of signal. In 1970 a new type of laser was developed, and the first optical fibers were commercially produced.

In a fiber optic communications system, cables made of optical fibers connect datalinks that contain lasers and light detectors. To transmit information, a datalink converts an analog (sound or pictures) electronic signal—as from a telephone conversation or the output of a video camera—into digital pulses of laser light. These travel through the optical fiber to another datalink, where a light detector reconverts them into an electronic signal.

## Fiber Optic Materials

Although small amounts of other chemicals are often added, optical fibers are made primarily of silicon dioxide ($SiO_2$) (a crystalline mixture like sand, quartz or flint). Liquid silicon tetrachloride ($SiCl_4$) in a gaseous stream of pure oxygen ($O_2$) is the main source of silicon for the vapor deposition method (explained in Step 1) currently in widespread use. Other chemical compounds such as germanium tetrachloride ($GeCl_4$) and phosphorus oxychloride ($POCl_3$) can be used to produce core fibers and outer shells, or claddings, with specific optical abilities.

Because the purity and chemical ingredients of the glass used in optical fibers affects the most important characteristic of a fiber—degree of attenuation (the amount of energy gradually lost)—research now focuses on developing glass of the highest possible purity. Glass that contains a high amount of fluoride (a highly corrosive, poison gas mixture) holds the most promise for improving optical fiber performance because it is transparent to almost the entire range of visible light frequencies. This makes the glass especially valuable for multimode optical fibers which can transmit hundreds of separate light wave signals at the same time.

## Design

In a fiber optic cable, many individual optical fibers are bound together around a central steel cable or high-strength plastic carrier for support. This core is then covered with protective layers of materials such as aluminum, Kevlar (a liquid polymer that can be spun into a nylon fiber), and polyethylene (a plastic) used for the cladding.

Because the core and the cladding are constructed of slightly differing materials, light travels through them at different speeds. As a light wave traveling in the fiber core reaches the boundary between the core and cladding, these differences cause the light wave to bend back into the core. Thus, as a pulse of light travels through an optical fiber, it is con-

### OPEN WIDE

*Doctors were among the first to find uses for optical fiber. Using an instrument called an endoscope they are able to peek inside the human body without having to cut it open. Endoscopes are narrow, flexible tubes that can be inserted in openings such as the mouth and throat. They contain optical fibers that shine light inside, and send pictures of internal organs back out. The tubes can also hold tiny surgical instruments and carry fluids or gases in and out.*

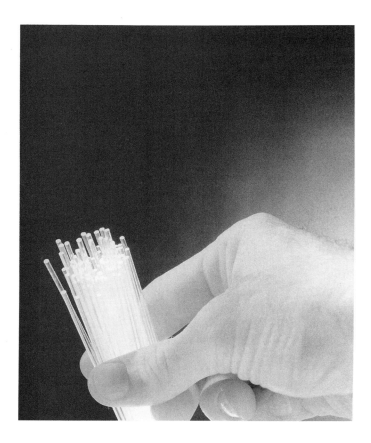

A pulse moves through an optical fiber at the speed of light—186,290 miles per second (299,340 kilometers per second).

stantly bouncing away from the cladding. A pulse moves through the optical fiber at the speed of light—186,290 miles per second (299,340 kilometers per second)—losing energy only because of impurities in the glass and because energy can be absorbed by irregularities in the glass structure.

Energy losses (attenuation) in an optical fiber are measured in terms of loss (in decibels, a unit of energy) per distance of fiber. Typically, an optical fiber has losses as low as 0.2 decibels per kilometer, which means that after a certain distance the signal becomes weak and must be strengthened, or repeated. With current datalink technology, laser signal repeaters are necessary about every 30 kilometers (18.5 miles) in a long-distance cable. However, on-going research in optical material purity is aimed at extending the distance between repeaters of an optical fiber up to 100 kilometers (62 miles).

There are two types of optical fibers. In a single-mode fiber, the core is smaller, typically 10 micrometers (a micrometer is one-millionth of a meter) in diameter, and the cladding is 100 micrometers in diameter. A single-mode fiber is used to carry just one light wave over very long distances. Bundles of single-mode optical fibers are used in long-distance telephone lines and undersea cables. Multimode optical fibers can carry hundreds of separate light wave signals over shorter distances. Multimodes have a core diameter of 50 micrometers and a cladding diameter of 125 micrometers. This type of fiber is used in urban systems (within cities) where many signals must be carried to central switching stations and distributed.

## The Manufacturing Process

Both the core and the cladding of an optical fiber are made of highly

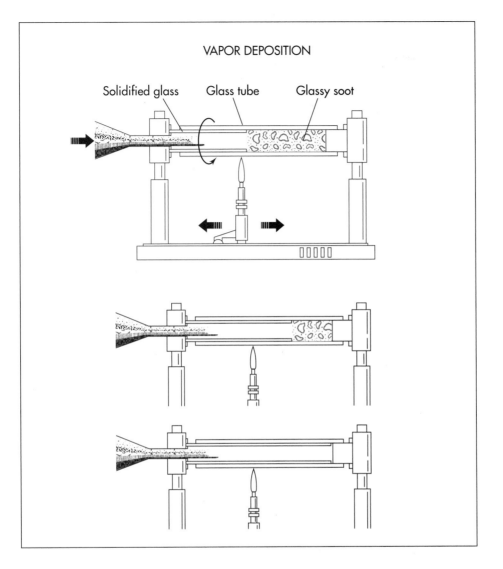

VAPOR DEPOSITION

Solidified glass     Glass tube     Glassy soot

Fig. 37. To make an optical fiber, layers of silicon dioxide are deposited on the inside surface of a hollow rod. This is done using Modified Chemical Vapor Deposition, in which a gaseous stream of pure oxygen combined with various chemical vapors is applied to the rod. As the gas contacts the hot surface of the rod, a glassy soot, several layers thick, forms inside the rod.

purified silica glass. An optical fiber is manufactured from silicon dioxide by either of two methods. The first, the crucible method, in which powdered silica is melted, produces fatter, multimode fibers suitable for short-distance transmission of many light wave signals. The second, the vapor deposition process (see fig. 37), creates a solid cylinder of core and cladding material that is heated and drawn into a thinner, single-mode fiber for long-distance communication.

There are several types of vapor deposition techniques: this section will focus on the Modified Chemical Vapor Deposition (MCVD) process, the most common manufacturing technique now in use. MCVD makes a low-loss fiber well-suited for long-distance cables.

## Modified Chemical Vapor Deposition

1 First, a cylindrical preform is made by depositing layers of specially formulated silicon dioxide on the inside surface of a hollow rod (see fig. 37). The layers are deposited by applying a gaseous stream of pure oxygen to the rod. Various chemical vapors, such as silicon tetrachloride ($SiCl_4$), germanium tetrachloride ($GeCl_4$), and phosphorous oxychloride ($POCl_3$), are added to the stream of oxygen. As the oxygen contacts the hot surface of the rod—a flame underneath the rod keeps the walls of the rod very hot—a very pure silicon dioxide is formed. The result is a glassy soot, several layers thick, deposited inside the rod. This soot will become the core. The characteristics of these layers of soot can be changed depending on the types of chemical vapors used.

2 After the soot builds up to the desired thickness, the substrate rod is moved through other heating steps to eliminate any moisture or bubbles trapped in the soot layers. During heating, the substrate rod and internal soot layers solidify to form the boule or preform of highly pure silicon dioxide. A preform usually measures 10 to 25 millimeters (.39 to .98 inch) in diameter and 600 to 1000 millimeters (23.6 to 39.37 inches) in length.

The fiber then continues through the machine, where its diameter is checked, a protective coating is applied, and it is cured by heat. Finally, it is wound onto a spool.

## Drawing the fibers

3 The solid preform is automatically transferred to a vertical fiber drawing system (see fig. 38). The machines that make up a typical vertical drawing system can be as high as two stories and are able to produce continuous fibers up to 186 miles (300 kilometers) long. This system consists of a furnace to melt the end of the preform, sensors to monitor the diameter of the fiber being pulled from the preform, and coating devices to apply protective layers over the outer cladding.

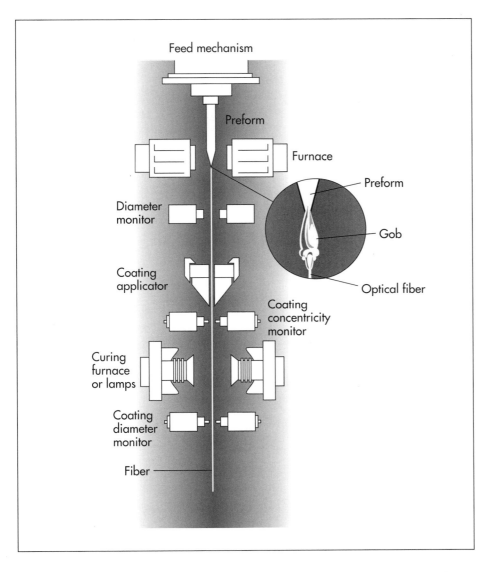

Fig. 38. After the solid glass preform is prepared, it is transferred to a vertical drawing system where the preform is heated. As it warms, a gob of molten glass forms at its end and falls away, allowing the single optical fiber inside to be drawn out.

4 The preform first passes through a furnace, where it is heated to about 3,600 degrees Fahrenheit (about 2,000 degrees Celsius). Next, a drop of molten glass called a "gob" forms at the end of the preform, much like a droplet of water that collects at the bottom of a leaky faucet. The gob then falls away, and the single optical fiber inside is drawn out of the preform. As the optical fiber is extracted, the material in

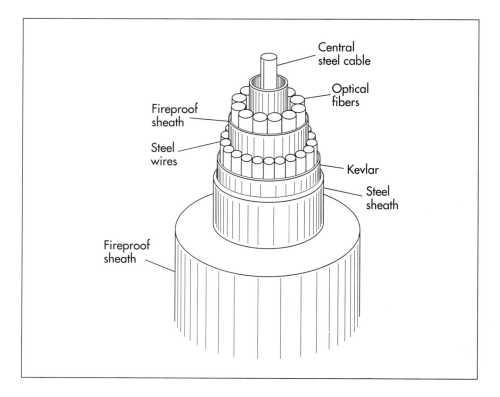

Fig. 39. A typical optical fiber cable usually includes several optical fibers around a central steel cable. Depending on the harshness of the environment where the cable will be used, various protective layers are applied.

the original substrate rod forms the cladding, and the silicon dioxide deposited as soot forms the core of the optical fiber.

5 As the fiber is drawn out, measuring devices monitor its diameter and the position of its center, while another device applies a protective coating. The fiber then passes through a curing furnace and another measuring device that checks its diameter, before being wound on a spool.

## Quality Control

Quality control begins with the suppliers of the chemical compounds used as the raw materials for the rods, and fiber coatings. Specialty chem-

The transatlantic optical fiber cable, known as the TAT-8, can handle 40,000 phone calls at any one time, which is triple the amount of calls that the seven existing copper transatlantic cables can manage together.

ical suppliers provide detailed chemical analyses of the compounds, and these reports are constantly checked by computerized on-stream analyzers connected to the process containers.

Process engineers and highly trained technicians closely watch the sealed containers as preforms are being created and fibers drawn. Computers operate the complex controls necessary to manage the high temperatures and high pressures of the manufacturing process. Precise measurement devices continuously monitor fiber diameter and provide information for control of the drawing process.

## Future Fiber

Future optical fibers will develop as research into materials with improved optical properties continues. Currently, silica glass with a high fluoride content holds the most promise for optical fibers, with energy losses even lower than today's highly efficient fibers. Experimental fibers, drawn from glass containing 50 to 60 percent zirconium fluoride ($ZrF_4$), now show losses in the range of 0.005 to 0.008 decibels per kilometer, whereas earlier fibers often had losses of 0.2 decibels per kilometer.

In addition to using more refined materials, the manufacturers of fiber optic cables are experimenting with improvements in production. Presently, the most sophisticated manufacturing process uses high-energy lasers to melt the preforms for the fiber draw. Fibers can be extracted from a preform at the rate of 32.8 to 65.6 feet (10 to 20 meters) per second, and single-mode fibers from 1.2 to 15.5 miles (2 to 25 kilometers) in length can be drawn from one preform. At least one company has reported success in creating fibers of 99 miles (160 kilometers), and the frequency with which fiber optics companies are currently retooling (replacing old equipment with updated tools)—as often as every eighteen months—suggests that still greater innovations lie ahead. These advances will be fueled by the growing use of optical fibers in computer networks, and by the increasing demand for technology in growing international markets such as Eastern Europe, South America, and the Far East.

## WHERE TO LEARN MORE

Billings, Charlene. *Fiber Optics*. Dodd, Mead & Company, 1986.
French, P., and J. Taylor. *How Lasers Are Made*. Facts on File, 1987.
Griffiths, John. *Lasers and Holograms*. Macmillan Children's Books, 1980.
Lambert, Mark. *Medicine in the Future*. Bookwright Press, 1986.
*Library of Science Technology*. Marshall Cavendish Corporation, 1989.
Macaulay, David. *The Way Things Work*. Houghton Mifflin Company, 1988.
Paterson, Alan. *How Glass Is Made*. Facts on File, 1986.
*Reader's Digest: How in the World?* Reader's Digest, 1990.

# Postage Stamp

## Stamp Starts

The postage stamp is a relatively modern invention, first proposed in 1837 when Sir Rowland Hill, an English teacher and tax reformer, published a pamphlet entitled *Post Office Reform: Its Importance and Practicability.* Among other reforms, Hill suggested that the English stop basing postal rates on the distance a letter traveled and begin collecting fees in advance of delivery. He argued that fees should be based on the weight of a letter or package, and prepayment be made in the form of stamps.

Hill's ideas were accepted almost immediately, and the first English stick-on stamp, which featured a portrait of Queen Victoria, was printed in 1840. This stamp, called the "penny black," provided enough postage for letters weighing up to .5 ounce (14 grams), regardless of its destination. To encourage widespread use of stamps, letters mailed without them were charged double at the point of delivery.

In 1843 Brazil was the next nation to produce postage stamps, which were printed by its currency (money) engraver. Various communities in what later became Switzerland also produced stamps in 1843. United States postage stamps (in five and ten cent denominations) were first approved by Congress in 1847 and became available to the public on July 1 of the same year. By 1860, more than 90 countries, colonies, or districts around the world were issuing postage stamps.

*Most early stamps were of a single color. The United States did not produce multicolored stamps until 1869, and they did not become common until the 1920s.*

Most early stamps were of a single color. The United States did not produce multicolored stamps until 1869, and they did not become common until the 1920s. The "penny black" and other early stamps needed to be separated with scissors; perforated stamps did not appear until 1854 in

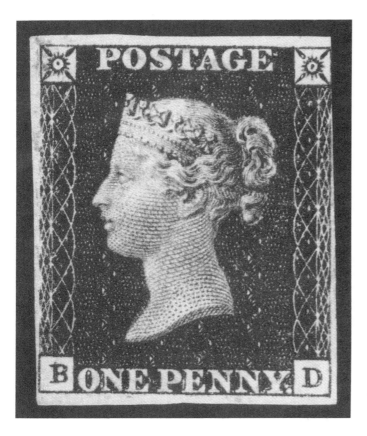

England's "penny black" (the first postage stamp issued by a government) and other early stamps needed to be separated with a scissors. Perforated stamps did not appear until 1854 in England and 1857 in the United States.

England and 1857 in the United States. Although larger stamps are occasionally produced, the penny black's original size, .75 by .875 inch (1.9 by 2.22 centimeters), has remained standard.

At first, stamps were manufactured by the same businesses that printed a country's currency, or by its "mint." Yet it soon became apparent that printing stamps is unlike minting money because the different paper types call for different printing pressures. Eventually, printing stamps became a separate activity. Over the years, methods of stamp production mirrored the development of modern printing processes. Today, stamp making processes use much of the finest printing technology available.

## Stamp Selections

In the United States, the decision to produce a stamp is made by a Citizens' Stamp Advisory Committee, a group of historians, artists, business people, and collectors, which meets regularly with employees from the Post Office. The committee is responsible for determining what stamps will be produced, in what denominations (amounts of money), and at what time.

Suggestions for stamps come from throughout the country, although the committee itself might recommend a particular design. The committee receives hundreds of ideas from collectors and special interest groups each week, although only a limited number of stamps can be issued per year. (If a person is to be honored by a commemorative stamp, the rule is that he or she must be dead.) In some cases, suggestions are accompanied by drawings and pictures which might help its chances of being chosen.

Once the committee decides that a particular stamp will be produced, it hires an artist to design it or modify a submitted design. It then decides, primarily on the basis of workload, whether the stamp should be produced by the U.S Government's Bureau of Engraving and Printing or by outside printers, who have been used much more often since the late 1980s. It's possible for a common stamp in great demand (such as an everyday first class mail stamp) to be made by the Bureau of Engraving and Printing as well as by several contractors. Currently, about ten to fifteen American firms are capable of manufacturing stamps that meet Post Office standards.

Elvis fans flooded the Citizens' Stamp Advisory Committee with more than 60,000 letters suggesting that he be honored with a commemorative stamp. More than 40 portraits were considered for the Elvis art work. The committee narrowed the field down to two, then, for the first time ever, asked the public to vote for their choice. The winner was "A Young Elvis," designed by artist Mark Stutzman of Maryland. The Elvis Presley stamp was issued in 1993 on January 8 (the singer's birthday).

Requirements for the stamp, such as color, size, design, and even the printing process itself are then decided with the original artist or designer. If the stamp is to be contracted out, a "request for proposal" appears in the *Commerce Business Daily*, a U.S. government publication which lists contracts available to non-government firms. After the stamp is printed, samples will be sent to the International Bureau of the Universal Postal Union in Switzerland, where they are marked as samples (commonly perforated with a word such as "specimen") and then sent to member nations to help postal workers recognize other countries' legal postage.

Other requirements, which can be met at a printing plant, are sometimes added to a stamp's design. The most common one is phosphor tagging, in which an invisible mark that can be read only by a special machine is placed on a stamp. The tagging helps speed the automated (machine) sorting of mail.

Another requirement might be for printing the stamp on chalked paper to prevent reuse of a stamp by cleaning or washing off a cancellation mark. When a canceled stamp printed on chalked paper is wetted, the picture will blur as the cancellation mark is wiped off, alerting postal workers to the fact that the stamp is no longer valid.

## Stamp Materials

Although stamps were originally printed on sheets of paper that were

The popular "Young Elvis" stamp.

fed into presses individually, the paper now used comes on a roll. The two kinds of paper most commonly used to print stamps are laid and wove paper. Laid paper has alternating light and dark lines visible when held to the light. Wove paper shows no lines. While other nations use both types, the United States presently uses only wove. Both types of paper often feature watermarks—faint designs that are pressed into stamp paper during the production process. Common in other countries, water-marked paper has not been used in the United States since 1915.

## The Manufacturing Process

At the printing plant, production begins when the stamp paper is

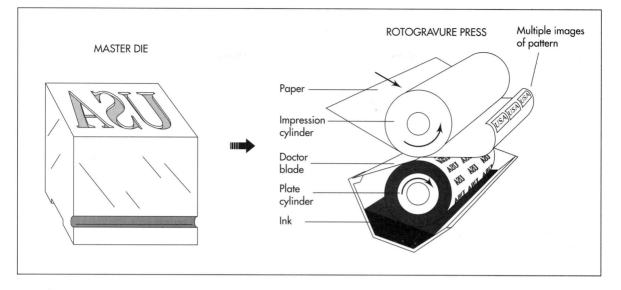

MASTER DIE

ROTOGRAVURE PRESS

Multiple images of pattern

Paper

Impression cylinder

Doctor blade

Plate cylinder

Ink

Fig. 40. The engraving method of intaglio printing begins with the creation of a master die (mold) on which the design of the stamp is engraved, in reverse. The master die impression is then copied onto a transfer roll, and then onto a printing plate. Next, the plate is inserted into the printing press and coated with ink, and the appropriate paper is fed through the press.

delivered, with the glue already applied to the back. Two printing processes are most often used in making stamps, the intaglio process (which includes the gravure process), and the offset process. It is not unusual, however, for a particular stamp's design to call for the use of both methods.

Intaglio, perhaps the oldest means of producing stamps, is also the most time-consuming. Because this method produces stamps with more distinct images, the process has not been abandoned for newer, faster, and less expensive methods. Intaglio involves engraving, scratching, or etching an image onto a printing plate, which in turn transfers that image onto paper. In one well-known intaglio process, called gravure, the image is transferred onto the plate photographically, then etched into the plate. This section, however, will first focus on an engraving process.

*The study and collection of stamps and postal materials (postcards, stationery, etc.) is called philately. The people who collect them are called philatelists.*

## Creating the master die

1 The engraving method of intaglio begins with the creation of a "master die" in which the design of the stamp is engraved, in reverse (see fig. 40). The design is in the lowered portion of the die (or mold)—

the raised portion of the die will not be reproduced in the final product. This is an exacting hand process, in which the engraver carefully cuts a mirror image of the original drawing for the stamp. It might be several weeks before the engraver is satisfied that a perfect duplicate has been produced.

2 Once the die is complete, it is heated to harden the engraved image. In the next step, the hardened intaglio is placed on a transfer roll, which consists of soft steel wrapped around a rod-shaped carrier, or mandrel, and which resembles a shortened rolling pin. The transfer roll is machine-pressed against the master die, and rocked back and forth until the master die has created a relief (raised, or standing out from the surface) impression on the transfer roll. At this point, the relief is a positive impression (no longer in reverse). The process is repeated until the desired number of reliefs has been produced on the transfer roll.

## Preparing the printing plate

3 Like the master die, the transfer roll is hardened by heating. It is then pressed against a printing plate, leaving another relief, again in reverse, on the printing plate. If there are several reliefs on a transfer roll, all can be passed to the printing plate. Several printing plates can be made from the same transfer roll if the decision is made to use more than one machine to produce a particular stamp. The impression on the plate is in the form of grooves rather than a raised image.

4 Once the plate is ready for use, it is fastened into the printing press and coated with ink (see fig. 40). Inking is done automatically by several processes including spraying ink through small jets or moving an ink-covered roller across a plate. The plate is then wiped by a blade called the *doctor blade,* leaving ink only in the grooves.

5 The plate then presses against the paper, leaving a positive impression of the reverse image that was originally copied onto the master die.

6 If more than one color is used, the separate tints are handled by a process known as *selective inking.* A particular color of ink is applied by a piece of hard rubber that comes in contact with only the section

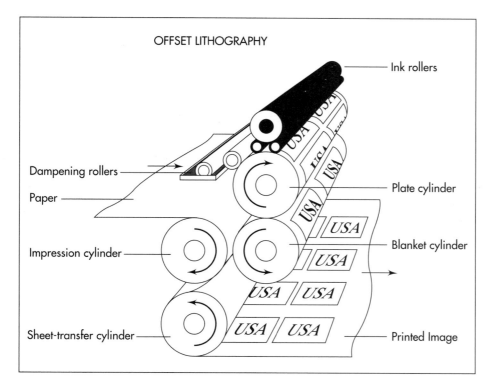

OFFSET LITHOGRAPHY

Ink rollers

Dampening rollers

Paper

Plate cylinder

Impression cylinder

Blanket cylinder

Sheet-transfer cylinder

Printed Image

Fig. 41. In offset lithography, a picture or design is made photochemically on an aluminum plate. Once attached to the printing press, the plate is alternately bathed in ink and water. Next, the plate presses against a rubber "blanket," which carries a reverse image of the final picture. In turn, the rubber blanket contacts the paper, producing the final positive image.

of the stamp that is to receive that color. After the ink is applied in one area, another piece of rubber, with another color for another area, is used to ink another portion of the plate.

## Offset lithography

7 The offset method of printing is less expensive than intaglio and can also produce very fine results, and it is a common choice for many stamps (see fig. 41). With this method, a picture or design is made photochemically on an aluminum plate. Once attached to the printing press, the plate is alternately bathed in ink and water: the photochemical image gets ink, while the non-image parts are dampened with water, which repels the ink and ensures that only the image will be transferred to the paper. Next, the plate presses against a rubber "blanket," which

carries a reverse image of the final picture. In turn, the rubber blanket contacts the paper, producing the final positive image.

## Perforation

**8** Perforations can be made either during the printing process by a machine attached to the printer or, less commonly, by a separate machine afterwards. With the first method, the sheet of paper is passed through a machine which uses little pins to punch lines of tiny holes through the paper in a horizontal and vertical grid. After pushing through the paper, the pins meet a matching metal indentation on the other side. After being perforated, the stamps move out of the press. In the other method of producing perforations, called *rouletting*, a wheel similar to a pizza cutter, but with pins, is rolled across one side of the stamped paper after it has been removed from the printing press, laying down a row of holes. Though originally done by hand, this method of perforation is now automated.

## Quality Control

Stamps are inspected at every stage of the printing process, by the people who run the machines and by inspectors whose sole responsibility is to observe the process and remove errors before the stamps proceed to the next step.

Printing machines are extremely complex, and errors in the printing process are a fact of life. Misfed paper, clogged inking parts, variations in pressure, changes in ink quality, incorrectly adjusted mechanisms, and a host of other problems can be minimized but not always eliminated. Even changes in the humidity of the pressroom can affect the press and the paper enough to produce less-than-perfect results.

Several of the most spectacular errors of the past occurred because presses were manually fed; in other words, individual sheets of paper were inserted into the press by hand. If a sheet of paper required an impression from a second press (to add a second color), and the sheet was turned accidentally, the resulting stamps featured misplaced blotches of color. This type of error does not occur today because presses are roll-fed: rather than being fed into a press sheet by sheet, paper is fed in from a continuous roll.

Stamp collectors love to spot errors—in fact, some philatelists only collect "mistakes," because an error can actually increase the value of

In 1918 William T. Robbey bought a single sheet (100 stamps) of Inverted (upside down) Jenny airmail stamps for $24. After realizing the post office's mistake, Robbey sold them to a dealer for $15,000. The dealer then sold them for $20,000. In 1979 a single Inverted Jenny stamp sold for $135,000 and continues to increase in value.

some stamps. Usually goofs come from the printing process. Occasionally factual mistakes slip in. In 1918 a U.S. airmail stamp featured an upside-down plane (see photo). In 1957 an Italian stamp designed to promote safe driving pictured a traffic light with the red light at the bottom rather than the top. Monaco issued a 1947 stamp honoring U.S. President Franklin D. Roosevelt in which his right hand clearly has an amazing six fingers. More recently embarrassed U.S. postal officials recalled and destroyed 104 million commemorative stamps that showed Black American cowboy Bill Pickett's name under his brother's (Ben Pickett) picture.

## COLLECTOR'S CLUBS

*Check the Post Office for a listing of local collectors' clubs, or for information write to:*

*Linn's Club Center*
*P.O. Box 29*
*Sidney, OH 45365-0029*

Most errors are caught quickly, and the flawed stamps destroyed, under tight security controls in the printing plant. Enough errors slip through, however, to make the collecting of "error stamps" an interesting specialty for some collectors.

## Future Stamps

One twentieth-century innovation that has significantly reduced the use of stamps is the postage meter. Developed in New Zealand in 1902, meters were introduced in the United States twelve years later. In addition to their use by the federal Post Office, meters are now leased by private companies that send out large amounts of mail. These meters allow companies to post and mail letters without using stamps. Particularly popular with businesses that send out bulk (large) mailings, meters now "stamp" over one half of the mail posted in the United States.

Individuals, however, continue to purchase postage stamps, which remain not only useful but popular. Stamps come in sheets, booklets, and rolled-up coils. Peel-and-stick, self-adhesive varieties are available for people who hate the taste of glue.

Stamp styles continue to tempt the tastes and interests of collectors all over the world. Stamp topics number in the hundreds and range from musicians, artists, famous people and events, to sports, science, transportation, animals, landmarks, and holidays. Most philatelists specialize in one or two types of stamps according to their personal interests. (For example, a sports fan might collect only stamps commemorating Olympic games or athletes.) Stamp collectors' clubs welcome new members and exist for all age groups in nearly every location.

### WHERE TO LEARN MORE

Briggs, Michael. *Stamps*. Random House, 1993.
*Introduction to Stamp Collecting*. U.S. Postal Service, 1993.
Lewis, Brenda Ralph. *Stamps! A Young Collector's Guide*. Lodestar Books, 1991.
Olcheski, Bill. *Beginning Stamp Collecting*. Henry Z. Walck, 1991.
Patrick, Douglas. *The Stamp Bug*. McGraw-Hill, 1978.

# Running Shoe

## Feet First

The average person expects little more of a shoe than comfort and style. Athletes are a bit more demanding. They want support, protection, and a little boost to their ability. Most shoemakers are happy to go that extra mile for a fleet-footed customer.

In recent years, the race to find the perfect running shoe has received about as much attention as the search for a cure for the common cold. Manufacturers, medical advisors, and runners themselves have focused on their feet in an effort to increase their speed. Why all the fuss? Because more people are racing, jogging, walking, and running for fun and fitness. As a result, the running shoe has changed dramatically over the past 15 years.

Running as a sport can be traced back to the ancient Greeks, whose culture was based on sound bodies and sound minds. During Greek athletic contests, runners competed barefoot and often naked. Later, the Romans insisted that their messengers wear thin-soled sandals. As shoemaking evolved through the centuries, leather became, and remained, the favored material because of its durability. The first shoes designed especially for running didn't appear until 1852, when historians noted a race in which runners wore shoes with spiked soles.

In 1900, the first sneaker, or all-purpose athletic shoe, was designed. Made mostly of canvas, this sneaker featured a comfortable rubber rim made possible by Charles Goodyear's 1839 discovery of vulcanized rubber. Goodyear gave rubber, an old product with limited uses, new life when he heated and combined it with sulphur. This vulcanizing process

*A runner's "footstrike" will land with a force equal to two or three times his or her weight. Athletic shoe makers try to soften the blow with midsole inserts of air, gel, foam, liquids, gas, plastic, even tiny rubber balls.*

Olympic hero Jesse Owens is reported to have worn Dassler shoes while capturing four gold medals in running during the 1936 games in Germany.

prevented rubber from hardening and losing its elasticity. In athletic shoes, rubber helped to cushion the impact of running on hard surfaces, but it didn't last long. Rubber was not strong enough for the tough treatment by runners, so leather made a fast comeback as the preferred material for running shoes.

But leather was far from an ideal material. In addition to being expensive, leather shoes rubbed a runner's feet raw. Runners had to purchase chamois (a very soft, cloth-like leather) as shoe liners for protection.

A Scotsman known as "Old Man" Richings provided some relief when he invented a customized shoe designed with a seamless toe box. This toe-saver was simply a piece of material inserted between the toe cap and the shoe lining and treated with a hardening substance. The toe box protects tender toes against rubbing.

In 1925, Adolph Dassler, a German shoemaker, decided to concentrate on athletic shoes, and founded a business with his brother, Rudolph, to do so. The Dasslers' running shoes provided both arch support and speed lacing, and their high-quality products attracted prominent athletes including some Olympians.

The Dassler brothers later formed separate companies—Adolph founded Adidas, and Rudolph started Puma. Another manufacturer of running shoes during the mid-twentieth century was Hyde Athletic of New England, whose specialty was football shoes. A 1949 description of Hyde's running shoe said it featured kangaroo leather, a welt construction (a welt is a strip used to connect the upper to the sole—see "Design" section), an elastic gore closure (a triangular piece of leather on the upper part of the shoe), and a leather sole covered in crepe rubber, a crinkly form of the material used especially for shoe soles.

One of the most unusual pair of running shoes in the mid-twentieth century were worn by the Japanese runner Shigeki Tanaka who won the 1951 Boston Marathon. Called the Tiger, his shoes were modeled after a traditional Japanese shoe that enclosed the big toe separately from the other toes.

During the 1960s, a company called New Balance began to examine how running actually affects the foot. As a result of this research, New Balance developed an orthopedic (based on a study of the skeletal system) running shoe with a rippled sole and wedge heel to absorb shock.

As running became more popular and joggers more demanding, the need for footwear that would help prevent injuries increased. Many runners began to request shoes that provided support in a lightweight construction. Nylon, invented during World War II, began to replace the heavier leather and canvas materials previously used to make running shoes.

Today the comfort of the running shoe isn't enjoyed only by joggers. Running shoes can be spotted on just about anyone who values comfort. Even formally-dressed office workers are switching to running shoes on the way to and from work. In 1990, consumers spent $645 million for 15 million pairs of running shoes, and experts note that the majority were bought for comfort rather than running.

## Running Shoe Materials

Running shoes are made from a combination of materials. The sole has three layers: insole, midsole, and outsole.

### BAREFOOT OLYMPICS

*Long distance runner Abebe Bikila of Ethiopia won the gold medal for the marathon in the 1960 Olympics in Rome. Shoe manufacturers around the world were horrified to see him accomplish this feat with bare feet.*

*The human foot has 26 delicate bones. Each leg has an additional 30 bones.*

Running shoes are worn also to be stylish.

*Many people have feet that are different sizes. If this is the case— always buy shoes to fit the bigger foot, then fill the extra space in the other shoe with a shoe insert.*

The insole is made from thin layers of a light, man-made foam called ethylene vinyl acetate (EVA).

The midsole, which provides most of the cushioning, varies among manufacturers. Generally it consists of polyurethane (a plastic, resin foam) surrounding another material such as gel or liquid silicone, or polyurethane foam given a special brand name by the manufacturer. In some cases the polyurethane may surround capsules of compressed air.

Outsoles are usually made of carbon rubber, which is hard, or blown rubber, a softer type, although manufacturers use an assortment of materials to produce different textures on the outsole.

The rest of the covering is usually a synthetic (man-made) material such as artificial suede or a nylon weave with plastic slabs or boards supporting the shape. There may be a leather overlay or nylon overlay with leather attachments. Cloth is usually limited to the laces fitted through plastic eyelets, and nails have given way to a glue known as cement lasting that joins the various parts together.

Running shoes have improved enormously during the last 15 years, and are now available in numerous styles and colors. Modern shoe designers focus on the anatomy and the movement of the foot. Using video cameras and computers, they analyze such factors as limb movement, the effect of different terrains (land surfaces) on impact, and foot position on impact. Runners are labeled pronators if their feet roll inward or supinators if their feet roll to the outside.

Along with pressure points, friction (rubbing) patterns, and force of impact, this information is fed into computers which calculate how best to adjust for these conditions. Designers next test and develop prototypes (models or experimental shoes) based on their studies of joggers and professional runners, readying a final design for mass production.

Running shoes are now available in numerous styles and colors.

A running shoe may have as many as 20 parts, and the pieces listed below are the most basic. The shoe has two main parts: the upper, which covers the top and sides of the foot, and the bottom, which makes contact with the surface.

Working around the shoe clockwise, starting at the front on the upper part, is the featherline, which forms the edge where the mudguard (or toeguard) tip meets the bottom of the shoe. Next is the vamp, usually a single piece of material that gives shape to the shoe and forms the toe box. The vamp also has attachments such as the throat, which contains the eyestay and lacing section. Beneath the lacing section is the tongue, which protects the foot from direct contact with the laces. Also attached to the vamp along the sides of the shoe are reinforcements. If sewn on the outside of the shoe these reinforcements are called a saddle; if sewn on the inside, they are called an arch bandage. Toward the back of the shoe is the collar, which usually has an Achilles tendon protector at the top back of the shoe.

The foxing shapes the rear end of the shoe. Underneath it is the heel counter, a plastic cup that supports the heel.

The bottom has three main parts, outsole, midsole, and wedge (see fig. 43). The outsole provides traction and absorbs shock. The midsole is designed specifically for shock absorption, and the wedge supports the heel. Located inside the shoe, the insole also contains the arch support (sometimes called the arch cookie).

## The Manufacturing Process

Shoemaking is a process involving a great deal of skilled labor. Each phase of production requires precision and skill, and taking shortcuts to reduce costs can result in an inferior shoe. Some running shoes (known as sliplasted shoes) have no insole board. Instead, the single-layer upper is wrapped around both the top and the bottom portions of the foot. Most running shoes, however, consist of an insole board that is joined to the upper with cement. This section will focus on cement-lasted shoes.

## Shipping and stamping the fabric

**1** First, prepared rolls of synthetic (man-made) material and rolls of dyed, split, and suede leather (used as part of the foxing) are sent to the factory.

**2** Next, die machines stamp the shoe shapes, which are then cut out in cookie cutter fashion with various markings to guide the rest of the assembly (see fig. 42). After being bundled and labeled, these pieces are sent to another part of the factory to be stitched.

## Assembling the upper and the insole

**3** The pieces that will form the upper part of the shoe are stitched or cemented together and the lace holes punched out. These pieces include the featherline, the vamp, the mudguard, the throat (with eyestay and lacing section), the tongue, reinforcements such as the saddle or arch bandage, the collar (with Achilles tendon protector), the foxing, and the logo. At this point, the upper looks more like a round hat than a shoe,

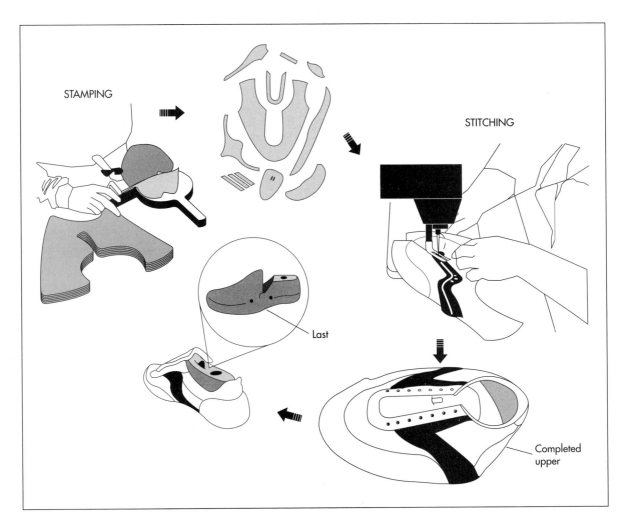

Fig. 42. The first step in running shoe manufacturing involves die cutting the shoe parts in cookie cutter fashion (a die is a tool used for cutting, forming, or stamping materials). Next, the pieces that will form the upper part of the shoe are stitched or cemented together. After the upper is heated and fitted around a plastic mold called a last, the insole, midsole, and outsole are cemented to the upper.

because there is extra material on the edges—called the lasting margin— that will be folded underneath the shoe when it is cemented to the sole.

4 Next, the insole is stitched to the sides of the upper. Substances to stiffen the heel area and toe box are added, and an insole board is inserted.

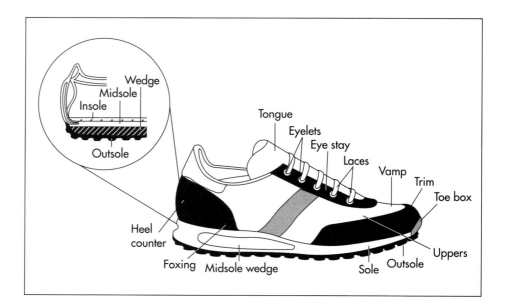

Fig. 43. Completed running shoes are quality tested using procedures developed by the Shoe and Allied Trades Research Association. The shoes are checked for defects such as poor lasting, incomplete cement bonding, and stitching errors.

### Attaching the upper and bottom parts

5 The completed upper is heated and fitted around a last—a plastic mold that forms the final shape of the shoe. An automatic lasting machine then pulls the upper down over the last. Finally, a nozzle applies cement between the upper and insole board, and the machine presses the two pieces together to bond them. The upper now has the exact shape of the finished shoe.

6 Pre-stamped and cutout forms of the midsole and outsole or wedge are layered and cemented to the upper. First, the outsole and midsole are aligned (lined up properly) and bonded together. Next, the outsole and midsole are aligned with the upper and placed over a heater to reactivate the cement. As the cement cools, the upper and bottom are joined.

7 The shoe is removed from the last and inspected. Any excess cement is scraped off.

## Quality Control

Manufacturers can test their materials using procedures developed by the Shoe and Allied Trades Research Association (SATRA), which provides equipment designed to test each element of the shoe. Once the shoe is complete, a factory inspector checks for defects such as poor lasting, incomplete cement bonding, and stitching errors. Because running can cause a number of injuries to the foot as well as to tendons and ligaments in the leg, another test is currently being developed to evaluate a shoe's shock absorption.

## Shoes of the Future

In the near future, experts predict small improvements of current designs and manufacturing processes rather than radical breakthroughs. Within the next ten years, athletic shoe sizing should become standard worldwide. Designers will continue to seek lighter weight materials that provide better support and stability with more use of gels and air systems.

"Computer" shoes are being designed with an electronic chip in the heel to measure a runner's speed, distance, heart rate, and calories burned. The chip is plugged into a home computer to read back the data. Another bright idea already shining on store shelves is the battery-operated lighting system designed to help the evening jogger navigate safely.

Good news for non-athletes: as consumers continue to spend millions for the comfort of running shoes, manufacturers will compete for these profits by applying running shoe design principles to everyday shoes.

### JUST DO IT!

In 1972 Bill Bowerman, University of Oregon track coach and co-founder of Nike, wrecked his wife's waffle iron by pouring urethane into it. Luckily no one tried to eat the rubbery result, and Bowerman's kitchen invention became a new outsole that outdid all the others for traction and comfort. Nike introduced the "Waffle Trainer" shoe the following year.

*Many quality shoe manufacturers add supports to correct the tendency of a foot to turn inward or outward. They help to keep a runner's feet on the straight and narrow.*

## WHERE TO LEARN MORE

Caney, Steven. *Invention Book.* Workman Publishing, 1985.

Panati, Charles. *Extraordinary Origins of Everyday Things.* Harper & Row, 1987.

Rossi, William A.,ed. *The Complete Footwear Dictionary.* Krieger Publishing, 1993.

"Running Shoes: The Sneaker Grows Up," *Consumer Reports.* May 1992, pp. 308-14.

*The Visual Dictionary of Everyday Things.* Dorling Kindersley, 1991.

# Salsa

*Most salsas are especially spicy, because of the hot chili peppers included in their ingredients. However hundreds of salsa sauces exist, ranging from extra-burning-hot to semi-sweet.*

## Salsa Style

Salsa is a spicy Spanish sauce that has become a popular side dish in the United States. In Mexico salsa is a sauce used as an ingredient for a variety of dishes or as a condiment (seasoning or dip). Most salsas are especially spicy because of the hot chili peppers used in the ingredients. Hundreds of such sauces exist, including piquant (a pleasant blend of sweet and sour) fruit salsas. In the United States, salsa resembles the spicy Mexican tomato sauce called salsa cruda, or raw salsa, and is used primarily as a condiment, especially with tortilla chips.

Salsas have been eaten for centuries in Mexico. The salsas available today are a fairly well-balanced blend of both Old World (European) and New World (American) ingredients. The tomatoes, tomatillos (a tart green fruit grown inside a papery pod), and chilies used for salsa making, grow naturally in this hemisphere, while the other ingredients, such as onions, garlic, and other spices, are of Old World origin.

Mexican cuisine (fine food) has traces of Aztec, Spanish, French, Italian, and Austrian flavors which arrived along with the early explorers and invaders. Though the ingredients of salsa come from places as varied as India and the Near East, most of them were staples in European kitchens before Spain's conquest of Mexico in the early sixteenth century. Most of the ingredients are a result of Spain's influence on Mexico.

Mexican meals often require time-consuming preparation. Traditional foods such as mole are complex blends of crushed spices, fruits, chocolate, and other ingredients that can take days to prepare. Fresh salsa was once made with the use of a molcajete and a tejolote, or mortar (a container in

A bowl of salsa surrounded by the various ingredients that make up this tasty dish.

which foods are crushed or ground) and pestle (a hand tool for grinding foods). This device, originally made from black basalt (a dense, volcanic rock), has been used to prepare a variety of foods for nearly 3,500 years.

## Salsa Ingredients

Mass-produced salsas bottled by large companies come in different varieties. The basic formula consists of tomatoes and/or tomato paste, water, chili peppers, (sometimes hot jalapeño peppers), vinegar, onions, garlic, green bell peppers, and spices, including black pepper, cilantro, paprika, cumin, and oregano. The most common alternative salsa is salsa verde, made with tart green tomatillos that replace red tomatoes in the basic salsa recipe. Other special formulas may use green tomatoes, carrots, black-eyed peas, or even cactus as ingredients.

Most commercially prepared salsas also contain additives, or extra ingredients to improve taste, appearance, and shelf life. These include salt, sugar, vegetable oil, calcium chloride (used as a preservative to pre-

*In 1991, salsa outsold the longtime favorite, ketchup, as the most popular condiment in America. Today, salsas account for almost half of the sauces sold in the United States.*

vent spoiling), pectin (used to jell the salsa), modified food starch (a carbohydrate), xanthum and guar gum (a natural substance used to stabilize foods), dextrose (a sugar found in plants and animals), and potassium sorbate. Beet powder and canthaxanthin can be added for color, and sodium benzoate or citric acid may be added as preservatives.

## The Manufacturing Process

### Selecting the produce

1 Salsa manufacturers purchase fresh, frozen, or dried fruit and vegetables, such as tomatoes, peppers, and onions, from growers. Other ingredients, such as vinegar, tomato paste, spices, or additives, are purchased from manufacturers in finished form.

### Preparing the produce

2 The tomatoes are first inspected, then peeled. The stems, seeds, and any left-over skin are then removed. Next, the chili peppers are inspected. Some salsa manufacturers roast their green chili peppers before washing them. After the stem, seeds, and leaves are removed, the chili peppers are blanched (scalded), and the pH value (or acid count) is adjusted using citric acid (from citrus fruits—lemon, lime, pineapple).

3 All other produce is cleaned by passing the vegetables through tanks of water or by spraying under high water pressure. The inedible parts of the vegetables (such as garlic peel, stems, or onion skins) are removed by processing machines. The vegetables are then cut using standard machines that are pre-set to the desired level of fineness. Salsas vary in texture and consistency ranging from chunky coarse to baby-food fine. To make chunky salsa, the vegetables are usually diced (cut into cubes) while the fresh cilantro (a leafy seasoning) is minced (chopped up very fine). To make smoother salsa, all the vegetables are processed and blended to achieve the same consistency as the tomatoes.

### Cooking the salsa

4 Due to long-distance transport of the product from manufacturing plants to stores, most salsa is not delivered fresh. Because the product must have a long shelf-life, heating the salsa is necessary to prevent the growth of mold within the container before purchase. Most salsa, however, is processed only for a short time. The tomato paste or

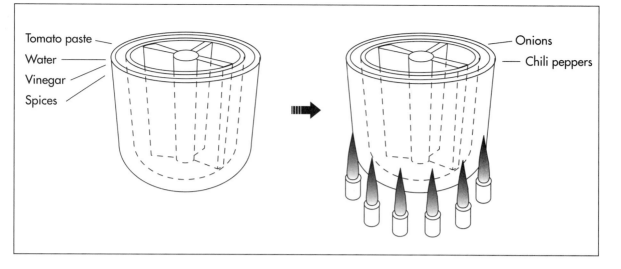

Tomato paste
Water
Vinegar
Spices

Onions
Chili peppers

Fig. 44.  Once prepared, the tomato paste or processed tomatoes, water, vinegar, and spices are placed in a pre-mix kettle that is large enough to hold several batches of salsa. This mixture is then placed in a batch kettle for cooking along with the other ingredients such as onions and chili peppers.

processed tomatoes, water, vinegar, and spices are placed in a pre-mix kettle that is large enough to hold several batches of salsa (see fig. 44). This mixture is then placed in a batch kettle along with the other ingredients such as onions and chili peppers.

Salsa may be slow or fast cooked, or, in the case of fresh salsa, steam cooked. Cooking time and temperature vary; the slow method cooks the salsa at a low temperature of 163 degrees Fahrenheit (71 degrees Celsius) for 45 minutes, while the fast method heats the salsa to a high temperature of 253 degrees Fahrenheit (121 degrees Celsius) for 30 seconds in a sealed container.

## Vacuum-sealing the salsa

5 After cooking, the salsa is poured or spooned into glass jars, plastic bottles, or other containers that are usually made from heat-resistant plastics (see fig. 45). Fresh salsa is placed into the container cold and then steam heated, while cooked salsa is placed into the container while it is still warm. A machine fills each container with the same amount of salsa. The jars or containers are then sealed and cooled by cold water or air. This process vacuum-seals the product because the heated salsa cools and contracts (shrinks), producing a partial vacuum under the seal. This vacuum,

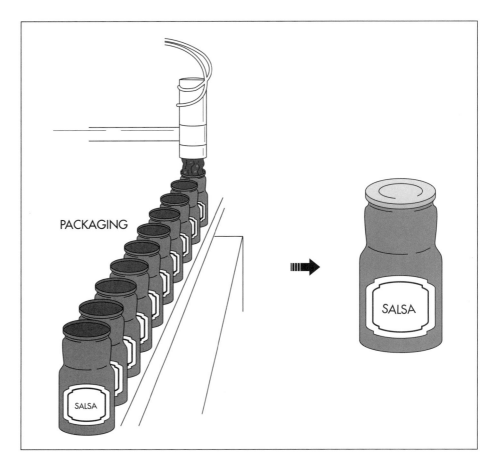

PACKAGING

SALSA

SALSA

Fig. 45. Salsa packaging is automated and uses large machines that vacuum-seal the glass or plastic jars after filling them with the appropriate amount of sauce. Salsa's surging popularity has made it the most popular condiment in the United States.

or absence of matter in the jar, pulls the top on tightly, and is the cause of the popping sound heard when a correctly sealed jar is opened.

## Packaging

6 Jars and plastic containers that are not preprinted with product information are labeled and packed in corrugated (layered and crimped) cardboard boxes to be shipped to stores.

## Quality Control

To assure consumers about the safety of the foods they purchase in

Salsa accompanied by tortilla chips and guacamole (an avacado dip).

grocery stores, the U.S. government requires food to pass a number of tests. This ensures that each batch is sterile and safe. Salsa manufacturers who do not use preservatives in their product must use even more care to prevent mold from growing during the shelf-life.

All incoming produce and spices must be inspected for quality. For mass-produced salsa, it is required that the vegetables be consistent in ripeness and quality so that batches will not differ in quality, color, or flavor. Consistency is especially important in chili peppers, as the degree of hotness must be within a strictly determined range.

Chili peppers are selected by choosing specific seeds or germ plasm (hereditary genes) appropriate for the salsa being made. Though chili peppers range in hotness—from the mild bell pepper to the hottest known pepper, the Scotch bonnet—most salsa manufacturers only go as hot as the jalapeño.

The system used to classify chili pepper hotness is the Scoville Units method. It determines the amount of water and time needed to neutralize

*A jar of salsa labeled "mild" should have a spicy flavor that won't overwhelm the timid salsa taster. A jar of salsa labeled "hot" should not disappoint the braver, fire-eating salsa consumer.*

the heat of the pepper after it is eaten. The higher the Scoville Unit, the hotter the pepper. The hottest chili peppers easily measure hundreds of thousands Scoville Units. Each type of pepper has several different levels of hotness to choose from, and the salsa manufacturer selects the peppers that will provide the necessary degree of hotness for each blend.

Once the salsa is prepared, it is sampled by experienced tasters to ensure that it meets acceptable standards of flavor and hotness.

The equipment used to prepare salsa is cleaned and inspected daily. It is cleaned with chlorides, strong ammonias, or any substance that is effective against bacteria, and then thoroughly rinsed. A swab test, which consists of rubbing a cotton swab over a small surface area of the kettle, is then done for each batch. The sample is placed in a solution, put on a dish, and placed in a laboratory incubator, and after one or two days, the sample is checked for microbes. The number of harmful organisms is multiplied by the total affected surface area of the kettle to arrive at the total number of microbes.

Many samples of the finished salsa are taken, and undergo the same treatment and testing as the samples taken from the equipment. Salsa factories are regularly inspected by the Food and Drug Administration (FDA), as well as state food regulatory inspectors.

Good salsa is a real test of the taste buds. A spoonful should stimulate the sweet, hot, salty, and sour sensors, one after another. American chefs are beginning to experiment with salsas, using fruity versions that substitute peaches or mangoes for the traditional tomatoes. And perhaps the best news of all— salsa-lovers can eat as much of the stuff as they want without worrying about nutrition. Salsas are quite low in calories (about six per serving), and relatively high in healthy vitamins and fiber.

## WHERE TO LEARN MORE

Birosik, P.J. *Salsa*. Macmillan Publishing, 1993.
Fischer, Lee. *Salsa Lover's Cook Book*. Golden West Publishers.
McMahan, Jacqueline H. *The Salsa Book*. Olive Press, 1989.
Miller, Mark. *The Great Salsa Book*. Ten Speed Press, 1993.

# Seismograph

## Chasing Quakes

The Earth as we know it today was shaped by the quakes and tremors of ages past. Movements of the Earth's crust, miles below the surface, cause wrinkles, bumps, and gaps above, which we see as mountains, valleys, hills, and cliffs. The land around us continues to change shape as the foundation below slips and slides—usually so slowly it can't be felt, but sometimes, with frightening, unexpected jolts that topple buildings and redirect rivers. Humanity has sought a means of predicting and protecting itself from earthquakes since early times.

Seismographs are instruments designed to detect and measure vibrations within the earth, and the records they produce are known as seismograms. The prefix for these words comes from the Greek term seismos, meaning "shock" or "earthquake." Although certain types of seismographs are used for underground research and exploration, they are best known for studying earthquakes.

A seismograph consists of a pendulum (an object suspended from a stable support so that it can swing back and forth freely) mounted on a support base. The pendulum in turn is connected to a recorder, such as an ink pen. When the ground vibrates, the pendulum remains still while the recorder moves, thus creating a record of the earth's movement. A typical seismograph contains 3 pendulums: one to record vertical movement and two to record horizontal movement.

## The First Seismoscopes

Seismographs evolved from seismoscopes, which can detect the direc-

A photograph of a strong-motion seismograph. The recording drum and film are located to the right; the starter, pendulum, and timing circuits are to the left.

tion of tremors or earthquakes but cannot determine the intensity (strength) or the pattern of the vibration. The earliest known device used to detect earthquakes was created by a Chinese scholar, Chang Heng, around A.D. 132. Detailed descriptions reveal that it was a beautiful and clever invention consisting of a richly decorated copper cylinder with eight dragon heads positioned around its upper edge, facing outward. Fixed around the lower circumference, directly beneath the dragon heads, were eight copper frogs. Each dragon held a small ball in its mouth that dropped into the mouth of the frog below it when a rod inside the cylinder, flexible and weighted at its upper end, was triggered by an earthquake. The particular frog that captured a fallen ball indicated the general direction of the earthquake.

For over seventeen hundred years the study of earthquakes depended on imprecise instruments such as Chang Heng's. Over the centuries a wide variety of seismoscopes were constructed, many relying on the detection of ripples in a pool of water or liquid mercury (the silvery,

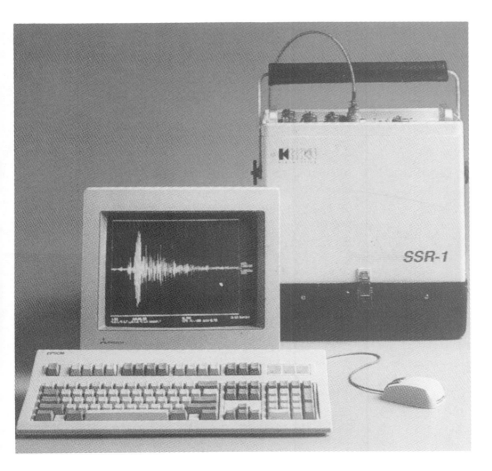

A modern field seismograph feeds a digital readout to a computer, which transforms the numbers into a waveform on its screen. Besides being portable, the field seismograph allows analysts to gather, handle, and store information more easily.

metallic liquid used in thermometers). One such device, similar to the frog and dragon machine, featured a shallow dish of mercury that would spill into little dishes placed around it when a tremor occurred.

Another type of seismoscope, developed during the eighteenth century, consisted of a pendulum suspended from the ceiling and attached to a pointer that dragged in a tray of fine sand, moving when vibrations swayed the pendulum. During the nineteenth century, the first seismometer was constructed. It used various types of pendulums to measure the size of underground vibrations.

# From Seismoscopes to Seismographs

The first true seismograph may have been a complex mechanism designed by the Italian scientist Luigi Palmieri in 1855. This machine used tubes filled with mercury and fitted with electrical contacts and floats. When tremors disturbed the mercury, the electrical contacts stopped a clock and triggered a device that recorded the movements of the floats, roughly indicating both the time and the intensity of the earthquake.

The first accurate seismographs were developed in Japan in 1880 by the British geologist John Milne, often known as the father of seismology. Together with British scientists James Alfred Ewing and Thomas Gray, Milne invented many different seismological devices, one of which was the horizontal pendulum seismograph. This sophisticated instrument consisted of a weighted rod that, when disturbed by tremors, shifted a slitted plate. The plate's movement permitted a reflected light to shine through the slit, as well as through another stationary slit below it. Falling onto light-sensitive paper, the light then "wrote" a record of the tremor. Today most seismographs still rely on the basic designs introduced by Milne and his associates, and scientists continue to evaluate tremors by studying the movement of the earth relative to the movement of a pendulum.

The first electromagnetic seismograph was invented in 1906 by a Russian Prince, Boris Golitsyn, who adapted the principle of electromagnetic induction developed by the English physicist Michael Faraday during the nineteenth century. Faraday's law of induction suggested that changes in magnetic intensity could be used to generate electric currents. Based on this idea, Golitsyn built a machine in which tremors cause a coil to move through magnetic fields, producing an electrical current which was fed into a galvanometer, a device that measures and directs the current. The current then moves a mirror similar to the one that directed the light in Milne's machine. The advantage of this electronic system is that the recorder can be set up in a convenient place such as a scientific laboratory, while the seismograph itself can be installed in a remote location where an earthquake might occur.

During the twentieth century, the Nuclear Test Detection Program made modern seismology possible. Despite the real danger to people and property caused by earthquakes, seismologists did not use a large number of seismographs until the threat of underground nuclear explosions prompted the establishment of the World-Wide Standardized Seismograph Network (WWSSN) in 1960. The Network set up 120 seismographs in 60 countries.

Developed after World War II, the Press-Ewing seismograph enabled researchers to record long-period seismic waves—vibrations that travel long distances at relatively slow speeds. This seismograph uses a pendulum like the one in the Milne model, but replaces the pivot (movable arm) supporting the rod with an elastic wire to reduce friction. Other post-war improvements included atomic clocks to make timing more accurate, and digital readouts that could be fed into a computer for interpretation.

*Scientists have identified two types of earthquakes. Strike-slip quakes occur when large plates (sections of the earth's crust) slide past each other horizontally in opposite directions causing the ground above to shift and shake. Thrust quakes occur in earth crust cracks where the edge of one plate drops under the other causing the ground around it to move vertically (up and down).*

The most important development during modern times has been the use of seismograph arrays (an orderly arrangement of machines and the data they produce). These arrays, some consisting of hundreds of seismographs, are linked to a single central recorder. By comparing the individual seismograms produced by various stations, researchers can determine the earthquake's epicenter (the point on the earth's surface directly above the origin of the quake).

## Modern Seismographs

Today, three types of seismographs are used in earthquake research, each with a period corresponding to the scale (speed and size) of the vibrations it will measure (the period is the length of time a pendulum requires to complete one full oscillation, or to swing back and forth one time).

Short-period seismographs are used to study primary and secondary vibrations, the fastest-moving seismic waves. Because these waves move so quickly, the short-period seismograph takes less than a second to complete one full oscillation; it also magnifies the resulting seismograms so that scientists can perceive the pattern of the earth's swift motions.

The pendulums in long-period seismographs generally take up to twenty seconds to oscillate, and are used to measure slower-moving waves which follow after primary and secondary waves. The WWSSN currently uses this type of instrument.

The seismographs whose pendulums have the longest periods are called ultra-long or broad-band instruments. Broad-band seismographs are used increasingly often to develop a more comprehensive understanding of underground vibration all over the earth.

The giant television screen and billboards at Anaheim Stadium collapsed during the 1994 earthquake in the Los Angeles, California.

## Earthquakes

Many areas of the world suffer from catastrophic earthquakes much more severe than those recorded in the U.S. The strongest U.S. quake shook Anchorage, Alaska with a 9.2 Richter scale reading in 1964. Next were 8.3 to 8.8 records set in New Madrid, Missouri (actually a series of violent quakes beginning in December 1811 and ending in February 1812) which resulted in landslides, and caused the Mississippi River to flow backward, actually changing its course. The quakes capsized boats, and rang bells in church towers as far away as Boston. The most famous U.S. earthquake struck San Francisco before dawn on April 18, 1906. It registered an 8.3 on the Richter scale, and ruptured gas and water lines that triggered a fire which destroyed most of the city.

## Seismograph Materials

The parts of a seismograph are standard. The most important material is aluminum, followed by ordinary electrical equipment composed of copper, steel, glass, and plastic. A modern seismograph consists of one or more seismometers that measure the vibrations of the earth. A seismometer includes a pendulum (an unmoving part) inside an airtight container that is attached to a grounded supporting frame by a hinge and a wire (for horizontal units) or a spring (for vertical units). One or more electric coils is attached to the pendulum and placed within the field (reach or force) of a magnet. Even the tiniest movements of the coil will generate electrical signals that are then fed into an amplifier and filter and stored in computer memory for later printing.

A less sophisticated seismograph will have either a mirror that shines light onto light-sensitive paper (as in Milne's seismograph), a pen that writes with quick-drying ink upon a roll of paper, or a heat pen that marks thermal paper.

## Seismograph Design

The demand for earthquake seismographs is not overwhelming. They are built by a few manufacturers who design custom-made seismographs to meet the needs of particular researchers. While the basic pieces of the seismograph are standard, certain features can be adapted to serve specific purposes. For instance, someone might need a very sensitive instrument to study seismic events thousands of miles away. Another seismologist might select an instrument whose pendulum has a short period of only a few seconds to observe the earliest tremors of an earthquake. For underwater studies, the seismograph must be waterproofed.

## The Manufacturing Process

### Choosing a site

1 A site might interest a seismologist for a number of reasons. The most obvious one is that the region is earthquake-prone, perhaps because it is next to or near a fault or fracture in the earth's crust. Such fractures, or cracks, shift one of the blocks of earth near them, causing the block to shift higher, lower, or horizontally parallel to the fault, and leaving the area vulnerable to further instability.

A seismograph might also be installed in a region currently without one, so that seismologists can gather data for a more complete picture of the area.

**2** Although some seismographs are placed in university or museum basements for educational purposes, the ideal location for earthquake research would be in a very quiet, less busy place. To record the earth's seismic movements more accurately, a seismograph should be placed where traffic and other vibrations are minimal. In some cases, seismographs are installed in an unused tunnel or a natural underground cave. Seismological researchers may even choose to dig a well and place the instrument inside if no other underground hole exists where a seismograph is needed. An above-ground seismograph is also possible, but it must rest above a solid rock foundation.

## Assembling the seismometer unit

**3** The working parts of the seismograph are assembled and prepared for shipment at a specialized factory (see fig. 46). First, the pendulum is attached to either a soft spring (if it's a vertical unit) or a wire (if it's a horizontal unit) and suspended within a cylinder between electric coils. Next, the coils are wired to printed circuit boards (PCBs) and placed inside the seismograph body. The whole unit can in turn be connected to a digital audio tape recorder, which receives the current generated by the coils and transferred to the circuit boards. If the data recording consists of more traditional equipment, such as a roll of paper and a pen, these are attached to the unit. Depending on the final destination, the seismograph is shipped by truck or plane in a cushioned crate by movers experienced in handling delicate electronic equipment.

## Installing the seismometer unit

**4** A seismograph intended for educational purposes might be bolted into the concrete floor of a basement, but research seismographs are best placed far from the inevitable vibrations of a building. They are either installed directly onto the bedrock (the solid rock under the earth's soil, sand, clay, and loose surface matter) where great precision is required, or in a bed of concrete. In both cases, earth is removed and the ground leveled (made flat). In the second method, a bed of concrete is poured and allowed to set.

**5** After the base has been prepared, the seismometer unit is bolted into place. In some instances where great sensitivity is required, it will be housed (encased) in a vault where temperature and humidity are controlled. The seismometer unit is usually installed in the chosen field,

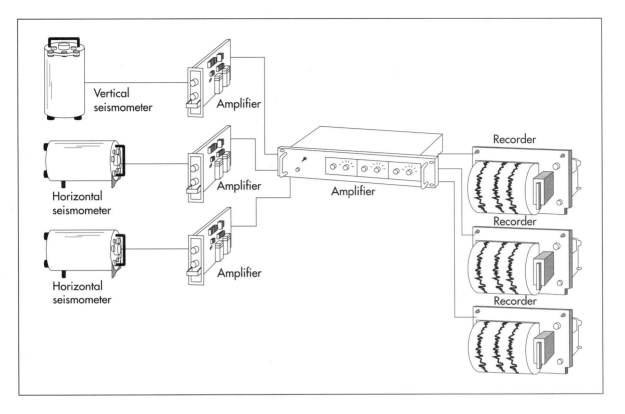

Fig. 46. A typical seismograph contains 3 pendulums: one to record vertical movement and two to record horizontal movement. The seismometer unit is usually installed in a field, cave, or vault, while the amplifiers and recording equipment are housed separately.

cave, or vault, while the amplifiers, filters, and recording equipment are housed separately.

6 In modern seismology, it is typical to have several seismometer units installed at regular distances from one another. Each seismometer unit sends signals to a central location, where the data can be printed out and studied. The signals may be broadcast from an antenna built into the unit, or, in more sophisticated units, beamed up to a satellite.

## Quality Control

Seismographs are designed to withstand the climate and geography of their surroundings. They are waterproof and dustproof, and many are designed to function in extreme temperatures and high humidity, depend-

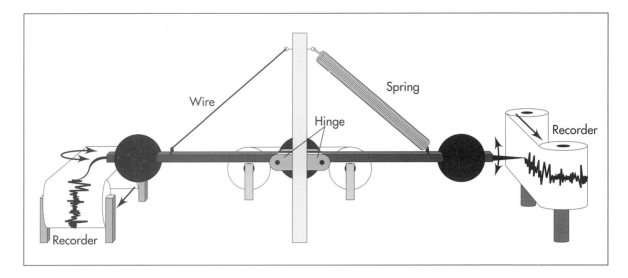

Fig. 47. While horizontal seismometers contain a pendulum attached to a wire, vertical units use a spring instead. When the ground vibrates during an earthquake, the pendulum remains still while the recorder moves, creating a record of the earth's movement.

ing on where they will be installed. Despite their sensitivity and protection requirements, many seismographs have been known to last 30 years.

Quality control workers in the factory check the design and the final product to see that they meet the customer's demands. All parts are checked for tolerance and fit, and the seismograph is tested to see if it works properly. In addition, most seismographs have built-in testing devices so that they can be tested after installation and before being used. Qualified computer programmers also test the software for bugs or other problems before shipment.

While sensitivity and accuracy are important, timing is also critical, particularly in earthquake prediction. Most modern seismographs are connected to an atomic clock that is adjusted to Universal Time (formerly called Greenwich Time), thus ensuring highly accurate information, understandable to researchers around the world.

Another critical aspect of quality control is minimizing human error. While earlier seismographs were simple, and practically anyone could learn how to use them, modern seismographs are precise, sensitive devices that are complex and difficult to use. Today, seismograph researchers and workers, if they are not qualified engineers and scientists, must be trained by engineers and scientists from the manufacturing facility. They must learn how to run and maintain the seismograph as well as the computer and other supporting equipment.

## Future Seismography

Seismology is best known for its use in the study of earthquakes. Emphasis has not been on study of the earth's internal structure, but rather on predicting and lessening the danger and damage of earthquakes in vulnerable regions. Study of the earth's interior has been directed toward searching for oil deposits, testing for ground instabilities before construction, and tracking down underground nuclear explosions.

Earthquake prediction, however, is of the utmost importance. If researchers can determine beforehand that a quake will take place, precautions such as increasing hospital and safety personnel can be prescheduled. But earthquake predication is still experimental. The first official earthquake prediction issued by the United States government took place only in 1985.

Recent major earthquakes, such as the one that occurred in San Francisco in 1989 and near Los Angeles in 1994, have intensified study of the famous San Andreas Fault in California. Currently, a team of seismologists is studying a smaller section of that fault to determine if they can predict a minor earthquake. The data from this attempt would be extremely useful in predicting major earthquakes in more heavily populated areas.

Other developments include more sensitive and more durable seismographs that can record both long- and short-period waves. One earth scientist believes that an earthquake warning system could be set up. Such a system would require a seismograph to pick up the vibrations, a computer to interpret them as a possible earthquake, and a communication system to warn emergency personnel in time. Some experts envision large groups of seismographs in earthquake-prone areas, where individual seismograph owners could collect and transmit data to seismologists.

## Future Shocks

So far seismologists have not been able to accurately predict future

### WHOSE FAULT IS IT?

*California is earthquake-prone because the earth's crust under the state is crisscrossed with faults (cracks). The largest is named the San Andreas Fault and stretches for an awesome 800 miles along its length from San Francisco down past Los Angeles. The San Andreas Fault separates two large earth plates, the Pacific plate which is very slowly moving northward (about 2 inches per year), and the North American plate which is slowly moving southward. Most of the time the rough edges of the fault catch each other and hold fast so there is no real movement. When enough pressure builds up between them, they will break apart or pull loose, slide past each other, and cause an earthquake or tremor above.*

earthquakes. In the mid-1970s Chinese officials successfully alerted and evacuated thousands of residents from the town of Haicheng before a large quake destroyed half its buildings. Unfortunately their warning system did not work the following year when an equally strong tremor leveled another city. While waiting for a dependable warning system, nervous Californians have enforced stricter building codes in an attempt to quake-proof their offices, homes, highways, and bridges.

## WHERE TO LEARN MORE

Golden, Frederic. *The Trembling Earth: Probing and Predicting Quakes.* Charles Scribner's Sons, 1983.

Knapp, Brian J. *Earthquake.* Steck-Vaughn Library, 1989.

Macauley, David. *The Way Things Work.* Houghton Mifflin Company, 1988.

*Reader's Digest: How in the World?* Reader's Digest, 1990.

VanRose, Susanna. *Eyewitness Books: Volcano and Earthquake.* Dorling Kindersley, 1992.

Walker, Bruce. *Earthquake.* Time-Life Books, 1982.

# *Sugar*

## Sweet Nothing

Human beings simply seem to have an instinctive craving for sweets. Even newborn infants will more readily drink water if it contains sugar. So why does sugar have such a bad reputation? Aside from causing tooth decay, its main fault seems to be a lack of nutritional value. The worst complaint health experts make about sugar is that it loads people up with empty calories.

## Origin

Before the birth of Christ, sugarcane (from which sugar is made) was harvested on the shores of the Bay of Bengal (east of the subcontinent of India); it spread to the surrounding territories of Malaysia, Indonesia, Indochina, and southern China. The Arabic people introduced "sugar" (at that point a sticky paste, semi-crystallized and believed to be an effective medicine) to the Western world by bringing both the sugarcane reed and directions for its growth to Sicily and Spain in the eighth and ninth centuries.

Later, Venice (the Italian island-city port of the Adriatic Sea) imported refined sugar from Alexandria (a city in northern Egypt on the Mediterranean Sea). Venetian merchants succeeded in establishing a monopoly (exclusive market control) on this new spice by the fifteenth century, and kept its cost quite high. Soon, shrewd Italian businessmen started buying raw sugar and sugarcane and treating it in their own refineries.

Venice's monopoly of sugar was short-lived. In 1498, when Portuguese navigator Vasco da Gama returned from India, he brought the

*Based on a 2,000 calorie per day diet, an average, unsuspecting person probably eats about 300 of those calories from sugars added to food. That adds up to about 14 teaspoons of sugar each day.*

sweet flavoring to Portugal. Merchants in Lisbon (the capital city of Portugal) noted the profits to be made, and started to import and refine raw sugar themselves. By the sixteenth century, Lisbon was the sugar capital of Europe.

It was not long before the sweetener was available in France, where its primary use was medicinal. During the reign of Louis XIV, sugar could be bought by the ounce at the apothecary (a specialty store for drugs and medicines). By the 1800s, sugar was still expensive, but was widely available to both the upper and middle classes.

The main ingredient (sometimes the only ingredient) in candy is sugar.

*Fresh vegetables as well as fruit contain natural sugar. As they age, the sugar turns to starch, and food loses some of its "fresh" or "sweet" taste.*

## Raw Materials

Sugar is a broad term applied to a large number of carbohydrates present in many plants and characterized by a more or less sweet taste. The primary sugar, glucose, is produced by photosynthesis (a plant's use of the sun's energy to make food) and occurs in all green plants. In most plants, the sugars occur as a mixture that cannot be easily separated from other plant matter. In the sap of some plants, the sugar mixtures are condensed into syrup. Juices from sugarcane (Saccharum officinarum) and sugar beet (Beta vulgaris) are rich in pure sucrose (common table sugar). Although beet sugar is generally much less sweet than cane sugar, these two crops are the main sources of commercial sucrose.

The sugarcane is a thick, tall, perennial (grows year-round) grass that thrives in tropical and subtropical regions. The sweet sap in the stalks is the source of sugar as we know it. The reed (stalk) accumulates sugar that amounts to as much as 15 percent of its weight. Sugarcane yields about 2,600,000 tons of sugar per year.

In sugarcane fields where the soil is soft, machine cutters cannot be used because they pull the plant up by its root. Since farmers expect the crop to grow back for another few seasons, they must harvest the reeds by hand in order to leave roots in the ground—a difficult and dangerous job. Sugarcane workers must wear heavy boots and aluminum guards on their shins and knees as protection from the long sharp knives used for cutting. It is "stoop labor" (meaning workers must bend from the waist to cut the stalks), monotonous and tiring. The sharp sugarcane leaves often cut or painfully poke the workers. Even so, the cutters are expected to harvest about a ton of sugarcane an hour.

*The human body doesn't care where the sugar comes from. The digestive system changes sucrose, whether from an apple, green beans, or a candy bar, into glucose (blood sugar) for energy. Glucose is the body's main fuel. Any extra calories from sugar not used up by exercise or other activity is converted directly into body fat.*

*White sugar crystals can be pressed into cubes, finely crushed, or pulverized further into powdered sugar.*

The sugar beet has the highest sugar content of any variety of beet root. While typically white both inside and out, some beet varieties have black or yellow skins. About 3,700,000 tons of sugar are manufactured from sugar beet.

Other sugar crops include sweet sorghum (another type of grass), sugar maple, honey, and corn sugar. The types of sugar used today are white sugar (fully refined—processed and purified—sugar), composed of clear, colorless or crystal fragments; and brown sugar, which is less fully refined and contains a greater amount of molasses, from which it obtains its color.

## The Manufacturing Process

### Planting and harvesting

1 Sugarcane requires an average temperature of 75 degrees Fahrenheit (23.9 degrees Celsius) and regular rainfall of about 80 inches (203 centimeters) per year. Therefore, it is grown in tropical and subtropical areas.

Sugarcane takes about seven months to mature in tropical areas and about 12 to 22 months in the subtropics. Fields of sugarcane are tested for sucrose (technical name for sugar), and the most mature fields are harvested first. In Florida, Hawaii, and Texas, standing cane is fired to burn off the dry leaves. In Louisiana, the 6- to 10-foot (1.8- to 3-meter) tall cane stalks are cut down and laid on the ground before burning.

Sugar makes cakes moist, cookies crisp, crusts brown, and helps yeast breads rise. It also helps baked goods stay moist and prolongs their shelf life.

2 In the United States, harvesting (of both cane and sugar beet) is done primarily by machine, although in some states it is also done by hand. The harvested cane stalks are mechanically loaded onto trucks or railroad cars and taken to mills for processing into raw sugar.

## Preparation and processing

3 After the cane arrives at the mill yards, it is mechanically unloaded, and extra soil and rocks are removed. The cane is cleaned by flooding the container with warm water (in the case of loose rock and trash clutter) or by spreading the cane on agitating conveyors (moving belts) that pass through strong jets of water and combing drums (to remove larger amounts of rocks, trash, and leaves, etc.). At this point, the cane is clean and ready to be milled.

When the beets are delivered at the refinery, they are first washed and then cut into strips. Next they are put into diffusion (softening) cells with water at about 175 degrees Fahrenheit (79.4 degrees Celsius) and sprayed

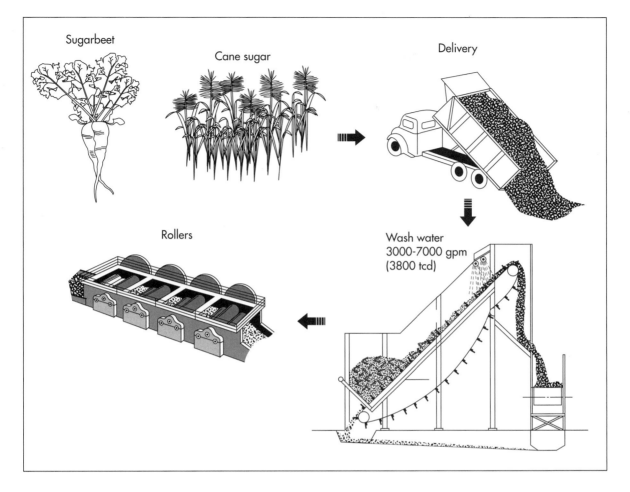

Labels in image: Sugarbeet, Cane sugar, Delivery, Rollers, Wash water 3000-7000 gpm (3800 tcd)

Fig. 48. In the United States, harvesting of both cane and sugar beet is done primarily by machine, although in some states it is also done by hand. The harvested cane stalks and beets are mechanically loaded onto trucks or railroad cars and taken to mills for processing into raw sugar. Once there, they are cleaned, washed, milled to extract juice, filtered, and purified.

with hot water countercurrently (from opposite directions) to remove the sucrose.

## Juice extraction pressing

4 Two or three heavily grooved crusher rollers break the cane and extract a large part of the juice, or swing-hammer type shredders shred the cane without extracting the juice (see fig. 48). Revolving knives that cut the stalks into chips supplement the crushers. (In most

countries, the shredder precedes the crusher.) A combination of two, or even all three, methods may be used. The pressing process involves crushing the stalks between the heavy and grooved metal rollers to separate the fiber (bagasse) from the juice that contains the sugar.

5 As the cane is crushed, hot water (or a combination of hot water and recovered impure juice) is sprayed onto the crushed cane counter-currently as it leaves each mill for diluting. The extracted juice, called vesou, contains 95 percent or more of the sucrose present. The mass is then diffused, a process that involves finely cutting or shredding the stalks. Next, the sugar is separated from the cut stalks by dissolving it in hot water or hot juice.

## Purification of juice—clarification and evaporation

6 The juice from the mills, dark green in color, is filled with acid and sediment, or particles. The clarification process is designed to remove both soluble (able to dissolve) and insoluble impurities (such as sand, soil, and ground rock) that have not been removed by earlier screening. The clarifying process uses lime and heat. Milk of lime (about one pound per ton of cane) neutralizes the natural acidity of the juice, forming insoluble lime salts. Heating the lime juice to boiling thickens the albumin (protein) and some of the fats, waxes, and gums, and this thick mixture traps any solids or small particles left.

The sugar beet solution, on the other hand, is purified by repeated infection of calcium carbonate (crystalline compound in chalk, limestone, or marble), calcium sulfite, or both. Impurities become entangled in the growing crystals and are removed by continuous filtration.

7 The muds separate from the clear juice through sedimentation (settling to the bottom of the liquid). The non-sugar impurities are removed by constant filtering. The final clarified juice contains about 85 percent water and, except for the removed impurities, is the same as the raw extracted juice.

8 To concentrate this clarified juice, about two-thirds of the water is removed through vacuum evaporation (see fig. 49). Generally, four vacuum-boiling cells or bodies are arranged in sequence so that each succeeding body has a higher vacuum (and therefore boils at a lower temperature). The vapors from one body can thus boil the juice in the next

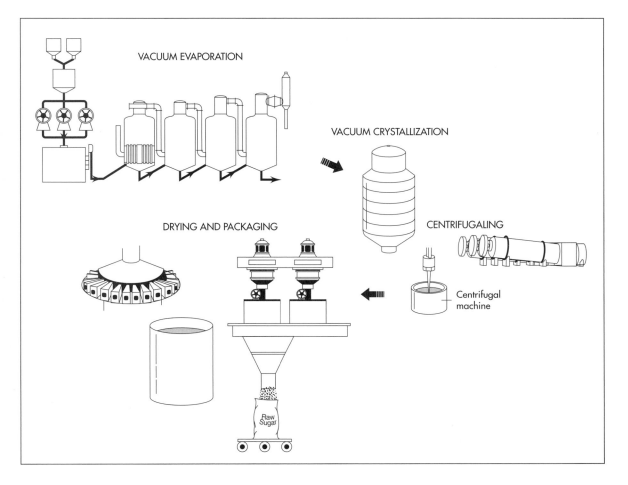

VACUUM EVAPORATION

VACUUM CRYSTALLIZATION

DRYING AND PACKAGING

CENTRIFUGALING

Centrifugal
machine

Raw
Sugar

Fig. 49. After being purified, the clear juice undergoes vacuum evaporation to remove most of the water. Next, the syrupy solution is vacuum-crystallized to form sugar crystals. The remaining liquid is removed using spinning gravity devices, and then the sugar is packaged.

one—the steam introduced into the first cell undergoes what is called multiple-effect evaporation. The vapor from the last cell goes to a condenser. The syrup leaves the last body continuously with about 65 percent solids and 35 percent water.

At this point the sugar beet sucrose solution is nearly colorless, and likewise undergoes multiple-effect vacuum evaporation. The syrup is seeded, cooled, and put in a centrifuge machine, which spins and separates materials of different density. The finished beet crystals are washed with water and dried.

## Crystallization

**9** Crystallization is the next step in the manufacture of sugar. Crystallization takes place in a single-stage vacuum pan (see fig. 49). The syrup is evaporated until saturated with sugar. As soon as the saturation point is exceeded, small grains of sugar are added to the pan, or "strike." These small grains, called seed, serve as a base (nuclei) for the formation of sugar crystals. Additional syrup is added to the strike then evaporated, allowing the original crystals to expand.

The growth of the crystals continues until the pan is full. When sucrose concentration reaches the desired level, the dense mixture of syrup and sugar crystals, called massecuite, is emptied into large containers known as crystallizers. Crystallization continues in the crystallizers as the massecuite is slowly stirred and cooled.

**10** Massecuite from the mixers is allowed to flow into centrifugals, where the thick syrup, or molasses, is separated from the raw sugar by centrifugal (spinning gravity) force.

## Centrifugaling

**11** The high-speed centrifugal action used to separate the massecuite into raw sugar crystals and molasses is done in revolving machines called centrifugals (see fig. 49). A centrifugal machine has a cylindrical basket suspended on a spindle, with perforated sides lined in wire cloth. Metal sheets inside contain 400 to 600 perforations per square inch. The basket revolves at speeds from 1,000 to 1,800 RPM (revolutions per minute). The raw sugar is retained in the centrifuge basket because the perforated lining retains the sugar crystals, and molasses passes through the lining (due to the centrifugal force exerted). The final molasses (blackstrap molasses) containing sucrose, reducing sugars, organic non-sugars, ash, and water, is sent to large storage tanks.

Once the sugar is centrifuged, it is "cut down" and sent to a granulator for drying. In some countries, sugarcane is processed in small factories without the use of centrifuges, and a dark-brown product (non-centrifugal sugar) is produced. Centrifugal sugar is produced in more than 60 countries and non-centrifugal sugar in about 20 countries.

## Drying and packaging

**12** Damp sugar crystals are tumbled dry by heated air in a granulator (see fig. 49). The dried sugar crystals are then sorted by size through vibrating screens and placed into storage bins. The sugar is then sent to be packed in the familiar packaging we see in grocery stores, in bulk packaging, or in liquid form for industrial use.

## By-products

Just about all the leftover materials (by-products) from sugar production are put to good use. The bagasse produced after extracting the juice from sugar cane is used as fuel to generate steam in factories. Increasingly large amounts of bagasse are being made into paper, insulating board, and hardboard.

The beet tops and unused slices, as well the molasses, are used as feed for cattle. More feed for cattle and other animals can be produced per acre per year from beets than from any other widely grown crop in the United States. The beet strips are also treated chemically to help with the extraction of commercial pectin.

The end product derived from sugar refining is blackstrap molasses. It is used in cattle feed as well as in the production of industrial alcohol, yeast, organic chemicals, and rum.

## Quality Control

Mill sanitation is an important factor in quality control measures. A small amount of sour bagasse can infect the whole stream of warm juice flowing over it with bacteria. Modern mills have self-cleaning sections with a slope designed to let the bagasse flow out with the juice stream. Strict measures are taken to control insects and other pests.

Because cane spoils relatively quickly, great steps have been taken to automate methods of transportation and get the cane to the mills as quickly as possible. Maintaining the high quality of the final sugar product means storing brown and yellow refined sugars (which contain two percent to five percent moisture) in a cool and relatively damp atmosphere that allows them to retain their moisture. Most granulated sugars comply with standards established by the National Food Processors Association and the pharmaceutical industry (U.S. Pharmacopeia, National Formulary).

## WHERE TO LEARN MORE

Burns, Marilyn. *Good For Me.* Little, Brown and Company, 1978.

Greeley, Alexandra. "Not Only Sugar Is Sweet," *FDA Consumer.* April 1992, pp. 17-21.

Mintz, Sidney W. *Sweetness and Power.* Viking, 1985.

Nottridge, Rhoda. *Sugar.* Carolrhoda Books, 1990.

Perl, Lila. *Junk Food, Fast Food, Health Food.* Houghton Mifflin Company, 1980.

# Super Glue

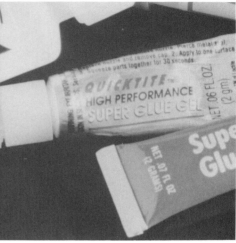

## Such a Sticky Subject

Glue is a gel-like adhesive substance used to form a surface attachment between different materials. Currently, there are five basic types of glue.

1. Solvent glues have an adhesive base mixed with a chemical solvent that makes the glue spreadable; the glue dries as the solvent evaporates. Most solvents are flammable (catch fire easily), and they evaporate quickly. Toluene, a liquid hydrocarbon made from fossil fuels, is the solvent most often used. Included in this category are glues sold as liquid solders and so-called contact cements.

2. Water-based glues use water as a solvent instead of chemicals. They work more slowly than chemical solvent glues, but are not flammable. This category includes such glues as white glue and powdered casein glue made from milk protein and mixed at home or in the shop.

3. Two-part glues include epoxy and resorcinol, a crystalline phenol that can be made from organic resins (thick, translucent substances found in plants). One part contains the actual glue; the other part is a catalyst or hardener. Two-part glue is very useful for working with metals. (Automobile dent filler is a two-part glue) but must be mixed properly to work well.

4. Animal hide glues are useful for woodworking and veneer work (bonding a thin layer of a material such as plastic or fine-grained wood over another material). Made from the hides as well as the bones and other portions of animals, the glue is sold either ready-made or as a powder or flake that can be mixed with water, heated, and applied hot.

*Cyanoacrylate glues are commonly called super glue. Usually referred to as C.A.s, these glues are the newest and strongest of modern glues.*

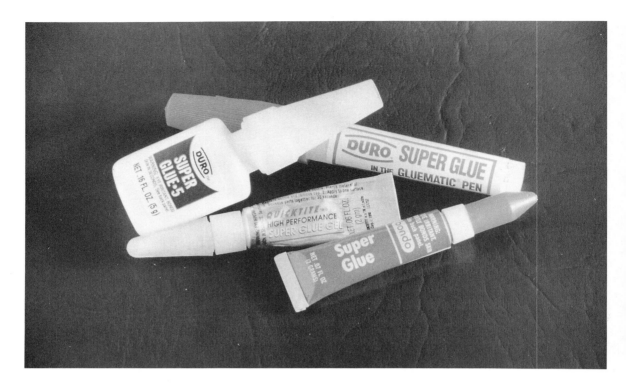

Various brands of super glue.

*Museums use super glue as a soak to strengthen brittle bones and fossils.*

5. Cyanoacrylate glues, usually referred to as C.A.s or super glue, are the newest and strongest of modern glues, which are made from synthetic polymers. A polymer is a complex molecule made up of smaller, simpler molecules (monomers) that attach to each other to form chains or chemical links. Once a polymeric reaction has been started, it can be difficult to halt: the natural impulse to form polymeric chains is very strong, as are the resulting molecular bonds—and the glues based upon them.

In the home and office, small quantities of C.A.s are useful for an almost infinite number of repairs such as mending broken pottery, repairing joints, and even holding together split fingernails. C.A.s have also become important in construction, medicine, and dentistry. This entry will focus on cyanoacrylate, or super glue.

## A Case of Serendipity

Cyanoacrylate glues were discovered at a Kodak lab in 1951 when two chemists, Dr. Harry Coover and Dr. Fred Joyner, were trying to find a tougher acrylate polymer for use in jets. Joyner spread a film of ethyl cyanoacrylate between two prisms of a refractometer to measure the degree to which it refracted, or bent, light passing through it. When he finished the experiment, he couldn't pull the prisms apart. At first, the unhappy chemists thought they'd only ruined a $700 laboratory instrument. They soon realized that they had stumbled upon a powerful new type of adhesive.

Moving from a lab accident to a useful, marketable product is not easy; Kodak did not begin selling the first cyanoacrylate glue, Eastman 910, until 1958 (the company no longer makes C.A. adhesives). Today, several companies make C.A. glues in a variety of forms. Some large manufacturers operate research laboratories in response to new demands for special forms and to develop new and better C.A.s.

The method by which polymers act as a glue is complex and not completely understood. Most other glues work on a hook-and-eye principle—the glue forms into microscopic hooks and eyes that grab onto each other, a sort of molecular velcro. With glues that work this way, the thicker the application, the better the bond.

However, cyanoacrylate glues appear to bond differently.

Current theory compares the adhesive qualities of the cyanoacrylate polymer to the electromagnetic force that holds all atoms together. Although a large mass of one substance will electronically repel (push away) any other substance, two tiny atoms of different substances placed closely together will attract one another. Experiments with several substances have shown that two pieces of the same material (gold, for example) can be made to stick to each other without any added adhesive, if forced close enough together.

This phenomenon explains why a thin film of C.A. glue works better than a thick one. A thinner glue can be squeezed so close to the material it is bonding that the natural electromagnetic force has a chance to take over. A thicker film permits enough space between the materials it is bonding so that the molecules can repel one another, and the glue will not hold as well.

*Car manufacturers and electronics firms are using super glues to bond plastic parts when metal bolts and rivets could tear them.*

## Super Glue Materials

The list of ingredients for super glue reads like a glossary of chemistry terms. Cyanoacrylate polymer includes the following chemicals: ethyl cyanoacetate, formaldehyde, nitrogen or some other nonreactive gas, free radical inhibitors, and base scavengers.

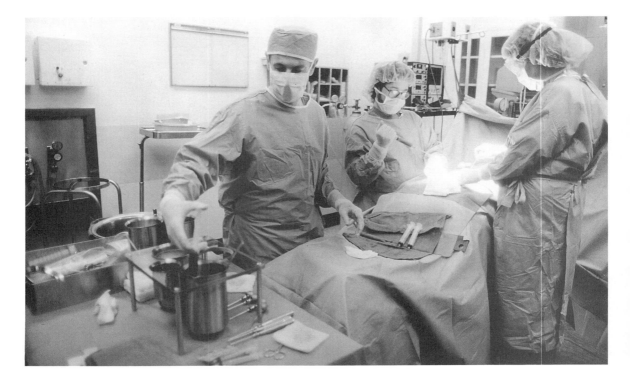

Doctors have used super glue in surgery to stop bleeding and seal wounds.

Ethyl cyanoacetate contains ethyl, a hydrocarbon radical (a radical is an atom or group of atoms that, because it contains an unpaired electron, is more likely to react with other atoms), cyanide, and acetate, an ester produced by mixing acetic acid with alcohol and removing the water.

Formaldehyde is a colorless gas often used in the manufacture of synthetic resins.

Nitrogen is the most abundant gas in the earth's atmosphere, making up 78 percent of air and occurring in all living tissue. Because it does not react with other substances, it is commonly used to buffer (separate or lessen the impact) of highly reactive elements that might otherwise clash when joined.

Free radical inhibitors and base scavengers serve to remove substances that would otherwise sabotage the product (keep it from working properly or hardening in its container).

## The Manufacturing Process

C.A.s are produced in heated kettles that can hold anywhere from a few gallons to several thousand gallons; the size depends upon the manufacturer.

### Creating the polymer

1 The first ingredient is ethyl cyanoacetate. Placed into a glass-lined kettle with revolving mixing blades, this material is mixed with formaldehyde (see fig. 50). The mixing of the two chemicals triggers condensation, a chemical reaction that produces water that is then evaporated as the kettle is heated. When the water has evaporated, what remains in the kettle is the C.A. polymer.

2 Because the C.A. will begin to cure, or harden, on contact with any moisture, the kettle space left empty by the evaporation of the water is filled with a nonreactive gas such as nitrogen.

### Separating monomers from the polymer

3 Next, the kettle is heated to a temperature of approximately 305 degrees Fahrenheit (150 degrees Celsius). Heating the mixture causes the polymer to crack. This cracking creates reactive monomers that will, when the finished glue is applied to a slightly moist surface, recombine to form a bond.

4 Because the monomers are lighter than the polymer, they evaporate upward and are piped out of the kettle into a second collector (see fig. 51). In going from one vessel to the other, the monomers move through a series of cooling coils that allow them to become liquid. A second distilling might be performed for a high-quality product, and some manufacturers might even distill the monomers a third time.

### Preventing curing

5 The contents of the second collecting container (the one holding the liquid monomers) are actually the C.A. glue, although they still need to be protected against curing. Various chemicals, called free radical inhibitors and base scavengers, are added to eliminate impurities

### A STICKY SITUATION

*Medical journals are full of painfully sticky stories about super glue. One sorry dad needed to have a plug of the stuff surgically removed from his ear after his 3-year-old son playfully squirted it there while dad was taking a nap.*

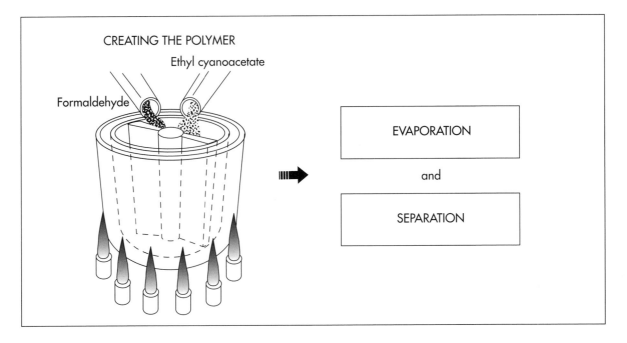

CREATING THE POLYMER

Ethyl cyanoacetate

Formaldehyde

EVAPORATION

and

SEPARATION

Fig. 50. Ethyl cyanoacetate, is placed into a glass-lined kettle with revolving blades and mixed with formalde-hyde. The mixing triggers condensation, a chemical reaction that produces water; this water is then evaporated as the kettle is heated. When the water has evaporated, what remains in the kettle is the C.A. polymer. Next, the kettle is heated again, causing cracking of the polymer and creating reactive monomers that separate out. When the finished glue is applied, these monomers recombine to form a bond.

that would otherwise harden the mixture. Because the quantities of impurities and chemicals used to remove them are small (measurable in nothing larger than parts per million), there is no need to remove them from the C.A. mixture. If these particles were visible, even under several hundred magnifications, it would be a sign of severe contamination, and the batch would be destroyed.

### Additives and packaging

6 The C.A. glue can, at this point, receive any additives that the manufacturer chooses (see fig. 51). These additives can control the viscosity (thickness) of the C.A. (in fact, at least three different thicknesses are sold), or they can help the glue to work on material types that earlier C.A.s could not. A thicker viscosity is desired when bonding is to be done on surfaces that don't meet very well; the thicker viscosity allows the glue to fill the empty spaces before it sets. Without other additives, C.A.s could only be used on non-porous surfaces (without pores or small

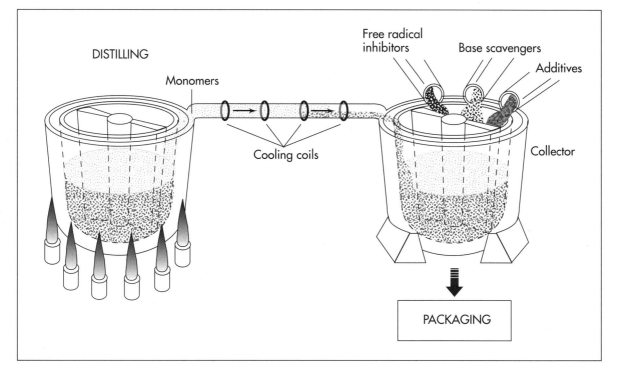

Fig. 51. The separated monomers are piped to a second kettle. In going from one vessel to the other, the monomers move through a series of cooling coils that allow them to become liquid. The contents of the second collecting container (the one holding the liquid monomers) are actually the C.A. glue, although they still need to be protected against curing. Various chemicals called free radical inhibitors and base scavengers are added to eliminate impurities that would otherwise harden the mixture. After receiving any necessary additives, the glue is packaged according to manufacturers' instructions.

openings). With additives in the C.A. or with some surface preparation, the C.A. will work very well. C.A. technology has allowed manufacturers to meet requests from customers for a C.A. that will bond almost any given pair of surfaces.

7 The C.A. can now be added to tubes using conventional, but humidity-free, techniques. Once a tube is filled, a top is fitted and crimped on, and the bottom of the tube is crimped (pinched or molded) closed. Because most metal tubes would react with the C.A., packaging tubes are usually made of a plastic material such as polyethylene, although aluminum tubes are possible. Once the C.A. is exposed to moisture or an alkaline, either in the air or on the surfaces being glued, the monomers will re-polymerize and harden, forming a tremendously

strong bond between the two substances. The reaction is total; the entire amount of C.A. that has been placed on the substances will polymerize.

## Quality Control

Careful quality control must be exercised if the product is to work properly. Because the polymerization of monomers is a universal reaction (it spreads throughout the amount of glue put on a surface, so that by the time the reaction has ended all glue has polymerized), a flaw in any step of the manufacturing process can affect thousands of gallons of material.

*Super glue bonds almost instantly, but it doesn't reach full strength for 8 to 24 hours. Wait the recommended amount of time before applying heavy weight or stress.*

Tremendous emphasis is placed on the quality of chemicals and supplies coming into the plant. Ideally, all suppliers have approved quality control procedures to ensure delivery of quality products to the plant.

Although the manufacturing process is automated, it is carefully monitored in the plant at all stages of operation. The duration of the mixing, the amount of mixture at each stage, and the temperature all need to be watched by operators ready to adjust the machines if necessary.

The finished product is also tested before shipping. Most important is shear resistance, a measure of the force necessary to break the holding power of the glue. Measures of shear strength commonly reach several thousands of pounds of force per square inch.

## Less is More

Many complaints were lodged against the first super glues. Customers were perplexed and disappointed to find that sometimes it worked great, and other times it failed miserably.

The secret to success with super glue is moderation. The thinner the film, the better it sticks. Also note the level of viscosity (there are several—thin, medium, and thick, at least) and match it to the job. For porous surfaces (wood, leather, pottery), use a thicker super glue so it won't just soak into the holes (pores) and disappear.

Additionally, curing times vary from two seconds to two minutes—but give the glue a chance to really set before testing it with heavy-duty stress.

Lastly, keep in mind that super glue bonds skin to anything with remarkable ease, so keep your fingers dry, and nail polish remover handy.

## WHERE TO LEARN MORE

Hand, A.J. "What to Know About Super Glues," *Consumers' Research.* November 1990, pp. 32+.

———. "Secrets of the Super Glues," *Popular Science.* February 1989, pp. 82-83+.

*Reader's Digest: How in the World?* Reader's Digest, 1990.

# Thermometer

## Weather Measures

Human attempts to accurately and scientifically measure the environment began with the invention of the thermometer. Despite the maps, graphics, and high-tech machines used by weather forecasters, a quick shift in the wind or a small change in the atmosphere can result in rain when sunshine was expected. Though weather prediction is a frustrating science, the measuring of temperature has proven to be a much more successful venture.

A thermometer is a device used to measure temperature. The thermoscope, developed by Galileo around the year 1592, was the first instrument used to gauge temperature. It was not until 1611 that Sanctorius Sanctorius, a friend of Galileo, invented and added a scale to the thermoscope, making it easier to determine amounts of change in temperature. By this time the instrument was called the thermometer, from the Greek words therme ("heat") and metron ("measure").

About 1644, however, it became obvious that this instrument—a large glass bulb holder with a long, open neck, that used wine to indicate the weather—was extremely sensitive to barometric (outside atmospheric) pressure. This pressure interfered with the accuracy of the instrument. To solve this problem, Grand Duke Ferdinand II of Tuscany developed a process to completely seal the thermometer from outside air, eliminating external barometric influence. Since then the basic form has varied little.

There are many types of thermometers in use today: the recording thermometer uses a pen on a rotating drum to continuously record temperature readings; digital readout thermometers that are often coupled

*Based on modern tests, many doctors think the "average" temperature of a healthy human is closer to 98.2 degrees rather than 98.6.*

with other weather measuring devices; the typical household thermometer hung on a wall or window, and those used for medical purposes.

With a thermometer, temperature can now be measured using any of three accepted scales: Fahrenheit, Celsius, or Kelvin. At one point during the eighteenth century, nearly 35 scales of measurement had been developed.

In 1714 Gabriel Daniel Fahrenheit, a Dutch instrument maker known for his fine craftsmanship, developed a thermometer using 32 (the melting point of ice) and 96 (then the standard temperature of the human body) as his fixed points. It has since been determined that 32 and 212 (the boiling point of water) are the scale's fixed points, with 98.6 being accepted as the healthy, normal body temperature.

Swedish scientist Anders Celsius, in 1742, assigned 0 degrees as the point at which water boiled, and

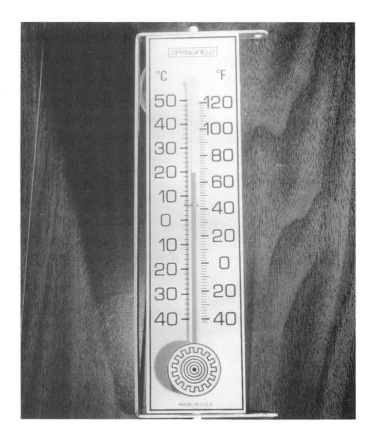

A typical household thermometer with both Fahrenheit and Celsius scales.

100 degrees as the point at which ice melted. These two figures were eventually switched—creating the scale we know today—with 0 degrees as the freezing point of water and 100 degrees as the boiling point. Use of this scale quickly spread through Sweden and to France, and for two centuries it was known as the centigrade scale. The name was changed in 1948 to Celsius in honor of its inventor.

In 1848 another scientist, Lord Kelvin (William Thomson), proposed another scale based on the same principles as the Celsius thermometer, with the fixed point of absolute zero set at the equivalent of -273.15 degrees Celsius (the units used on this scale are called Kelvin [K]). The freezing and boiling points of water are registered at 273 K and 373 K. The Kelvin scale is most often used in scientific research studies.

## Design

The operating principle of a thermometer is quite simple. Heat causes liquids and objects to expand (increase in size) and cooling causes contraction (shrinking). The amount of expansion and contraction is controlled by the amount of hot or cold temperature.

A measure of liquid, such as mercury, alcohol, or a hydrocarbon-based fluid, is vacuum-sealed in a glass tube. The liquid expands or contracts (rises or falls in a narrow glass tube) when air is heated or cooled. As the liquid level changes, a corresponding temperature scale is read which indicates the current temperature.

Thermometers are designed according to standards set by the National Institute of Standards and Technology (NIST) and standard manufacturing practices. It is possible to custom-design thermometers, but they must adhere to strict regulatory guidelines. Custom thermometers can be as varied as those who use them. The size and shape depend upon the length of glass to be used and the type of liquid it will be filled with. The placement of gradations (degree marks) laid onto the glass tube or enclosure, and even the color of the gradation scale marks are also considerations in custom-designing.

Use of electronic parts in thermometers has grown. Many of today's thermometers contain digital readouts and sample program cycles to feed back the current temperature to a light-emitting diode (LED) or liquid crystal display (LCD) panel. For all the electronic wizardry available, a thermometer must still contain a heat-cold sensitizing element in order to respond to environmental changes.

## Thermometer Materials

Thermometers consist of three basic elements: spirit-filled liquid (alcohol mixture),

A 1940s baby bottle with a built-in thermometer.

which responds to changes in heat and cold; a glass tube to house or hold the temperature-measuring liquid; and black ink to color the engraved scale marks with legible (readable) numbers. Other elements necessary for the manufacture of thermometers include a wax solution, used to engrave the scale marks on the glass tube; an engraving engine that makes permanent gradations on the glass tube; and a hydrofluoric acid solution (a corrosive substance used to etch glass) into which the glass tube is dipped to seal the engraving marks.

The glass material which forms the body of the thermometer is usually received from an outside manufacturer. Some thermometer products are made with an extra cover, which can be made of plastic or composites (combined materials) and may have the scale gradations engraved on them instead of on the glass tube. Along with providing protection, this cover also allows the thermometer to be mounted on a wall, post, window, or in a weather shelter box.

## The Manufacturing Process

Although there are numerous types of thermometers, the production process for the most common of these—the classic household variety—is described below.

### The glass bulb

1 First, the raw glass material is received from an outside manufacturer. The tube is made with a narrow passage, or bore, throughout its length (see fig. 52). The bored tubes are checked for quality; any rejected parts are sent back to the manufacturer for replacement.

2 The bulb reservoir which holds the fluid is formed by heating one end of the glass tube, pinching it closed, and using glassblowing and the application of an air-driven torch to complete it. The bulb can also be made by blowing a separate piece of lab material that is then

joined with one end of the glass tube. The bulb is sealed at the bottom, leaving an open tube at the top.

### Adding the fluid

3 With the open end placed down in a vacuum chamber, air is then taken out of the glass tube, and the hydrocarbon fluid (hydrogen and carbon) enters the vacuum until it penetrates the tube about 1 inch (2.54 centimeters) (see fig. 52). Due to environmental concerns, modern thermometers are manufactured less with mercury and more with a spirit-filled (alcohol solution) hydrocarbon liquid. Such a practice is required (with tolerance for a limited use of mercury) by the Environmental Protection Agency (EPA).

The vacuum is then gradually reduced, forcing the fluid down to the top of the tube. The process is the same when mercury is used, except that heat is also applied in the vacuum chamber.

4 Once full, the tube is placed upon the bulb end. A heating-out process is then conducted by placing the thermometer into a warm bath and raising the temperature to 400 degrees Fahrenheit (204 degrees Celsius). Next, the temperature is reduced to room temperature to bring the remaining liquid back to a known level. The open end of the thermometer is then sealed by placing it over a flame.

### Applying the scale

5 After the tube is sealed, a scale is applied, based on the level at which the fluid rests when inserted into a boiling water bath of 212 degrees Fahrenheit (100 degrees Celsius) versus one at the freezing temperature of 32 degrees Fahrenheit (0 degrees Celsius) (see fig. 53). These reference points for the desired scale are marked on the glass tube before engraving or silkscreening is done to mark the rest of the degrees.

6 The range lengths vary according to the design used. A scale is chosen that best corresponds to even marks between the reference points (freezing and boiling). For accuracy purposes, engraving is the preferred method of marking. The marks are made by an engraving engine after the thermometer is placed in wax. The numbers are scratched onto the glass and, once completed, the thermometer is dipped in hydro-

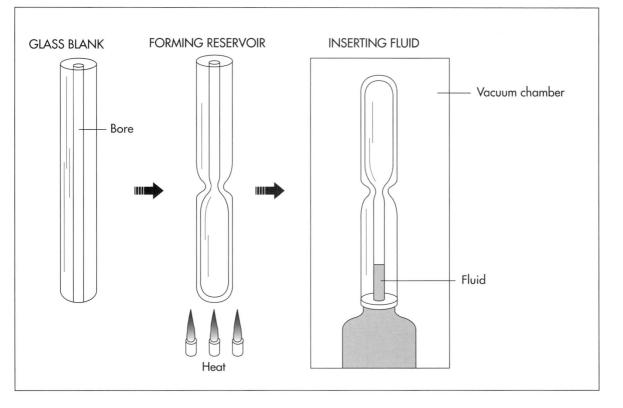

GLASS BLANK  FORMING RESERVOIR  INSERTING FLUID

Bore

Vacuum chamber

Fluid

Heat

Fig. 52. Thermometer manufacturers start with glass blanks with bores (narrow openings) down the middle. The bulb reservoir is formed by heating one end of the glass tube and pinching it closed. The bulb is sealed at the bottom, leaving an open tube at the top. Next, the open end is tipped down in a vacuum chamber, air is taken out of the glass tube, and a hydrocarbon (hydrogen and carbon) fluid enters the vacuum until it penetrates the tube about 1 inch.

fluoric acid to seal the engraved markings. Ink is then rubbed into the marks to highlight the scale values. When covers are used on the scales, a silkscreening process is used to apply the marks.

7 Finally, the thermometers are packaged according to manufacturers' designs and shipped to customers.

## Quality Control

The manufacturing process is controlled by accepted industry standards and specific in-house measures. Manufacturing design considera-

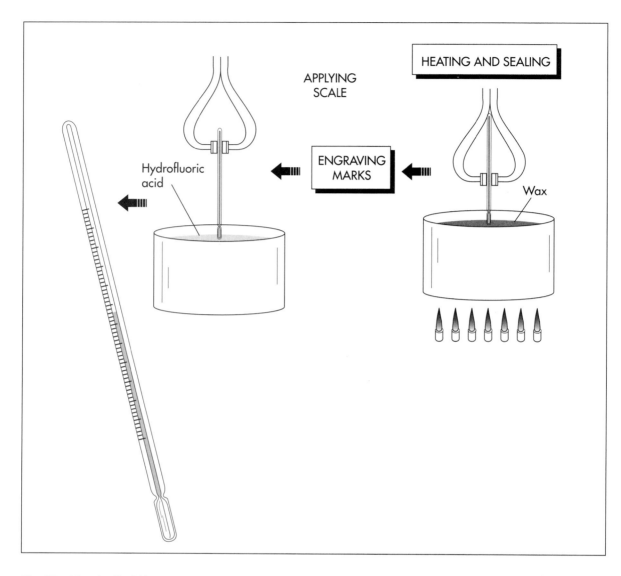

APPLYING
SCALE

**HEATING AND SEALING**

Hydrofluoric
acid

ENGRAVING
MARKS

Wax

Fig. 53. After the liquid inserted, the unit is heated and sealed. Next, the scale markings are added. This is done by engraving, in which the bulb is dipped in wax, the marks engraved, and the bulb dipped in hydrofluoric acid to seal the marks on the glass.

tions include quality control checks throughout the production process. Production equipment must also be carefully maintained, especially with updated design requirements (for digital and electronic thermometers).

Waste materials collected during manufacturing are disposed of according to environmental regulatory standards. During the manufacturing cycle, equipment used to heat, empty, and engrave the thermometer must be checked and calibrated (measured and standardized) regularly. Tolerance tests are also performed, using a known standard, to determine the accuracy of the temperature readings. All thermometers have a tolerance (allowance) for accuracy. For the common household, this tolerance is usually plus or minus 2 degrees Fahrenheit (16 degrees Celsius). For laboratory work, plus or minus 1 degree is generally acceptable.

## Future Thermometers

Although the traditional simple glass thermometer is unlikely to change, other thermometer designs continue to evolve. With technological advances and more widespread use of lighter and stronger materials, manufacturers of electronic temperature instruments can provide more accurate measurements with smaller equipment at an affordable price.

Digital thermometers use a computer chip instead of fluid to measure temperature and translate it into degrees. Body temperature can be measured in less than a minute—no small advantage when the patient is a very young, restless child—and easily read from a liquid crystal display (LCD). Most digital thermometers are about the size of a pen or marker, made of unbreakable plastic, and are powered by a tiny battery which usually lasts for more than a year.

Analog box thermometers were once used with a long wire and probe tip for in-ground temperature measurements. Today, the probe tips are made of lighter materials, and the boxes, loaded with digital electronics, are not as bulky and square. It may eventually be possible to direct an infrared beam into soil and extract a temperature reading from a target depth without even touching the soil.

## WHERE TO LEARN MORE

Gardner, Robert. *Temperature and Heat*. Simon & Schuster, 1993.
Macaulay, David. *The Way Things Work*. Houghton Mifflin Company, 1988.
Meehan, Beth Ann. "Body Heat," *Discover*. January 1993, pp. 52-53.
Parker, Steve. *Eyewitness Science: Electricity*. Dorling Kindersley, 1992.
Rocoznica, June. "Fast Fever Readings," *Health*. March 1990, p. 38+.

# Tire

## Tire Tracks

Shortly after the revolutionary and time-saving invention of the wheel, cavemen began to complain about its rough ride. Tires came to the rescue with a comfortable cushion of rubber and air—but not until many centuries later.

A tire is a strong, flexible rubber casing attached to the rim of a wheel. Tires provide a gripping surface for traction and serve as a cushion for the wheels of a moving vehicle. Tires are found on bicycles, baby carriages, shopping carts, wheel chairs, motorcycles, automobiles, trucks, buses, aircraft, tractors, and industrial vehicles.

Tires for most vehicles are pneumatic, that is, filled with pressurized air. Until recently, pneumatic tires had an inner tube to hold the air pressure, but now they are designed to form a pressure seal with the rim of the wheel.

## Origin

Scottish inventor Robert Thomson developed the pneumatic tire with inner tube in 1845. Unfortunately his design was far ahead of its time and attracted little interest. The pneumatic tire was reinvented in the 1880s by another Scotsman, John Boyd Dunlop, and was an instant success with bicyclists.

Natural rubber is the main raw material used in manufacturing tires, although synthetic (man-made) rubber is also used. In order to develop the proper characteristics of strength, resiliency, and wear-resistance, however, the rubber must be treated with a variety of chemicals and then heated.

*Scottish inventor Robert Thomson developed the pneumatic tire with inner tube in 1845 but attracted little interest. The tire was reinvented in the 1880s by John Boyd Dunlop and was an instant success with bicyclists.*

American inventor Charles Goodyear accidentally discovered the process of strengthening rubber, known as vulcanization or curing in 1839. He had been experimenting with rubber since 1830 but had been unable to develop a suitable curing process. During an experiment with a mixture of india rubber and sulfur, Goodyear dropped the mixture on a hot stove. A chemical reaction took place and, instead of melting, the rubber-sulfur mixture formed a hard lump. He continued his experiments until he could treat continuous sheets of rubber.

Today, large, efficient factories staffed with skilled workers produce more than 250 million new tires a year. Although automation guides many of the steps in the manufacturing process, skilled workers are still required to assemble the parts of a tire.

A typical bicycle tire.

## Tire Materials

Rubber is the main raw material used in manufacturing tires, and both natural and synthetic rubber are used. Natural rubber is found as a milky liquid in the bark of the rubber tree, Hevea Brasiliensis. To produce the raw rubber used in tire manufacturing, the liquid latex (milky sap of the rubber tree) is mixed with acids that cause the rubber to become solid. Presses squeeze out excess water and form the rubber into sheets. The sheets are then dried in tall smokehouses, pressed into enormous bales, and shipped to tire factories around the world. Synthetic rubber is produced from the polymers (chains of molecules) found in crude oil.

The other primary ingredient in tire rubber is carbon black. Carbon black is a fine, soft powder produced when crude oil or natural gas is burned with a limited amount of oxygen, creating a large amount of fine soot. So much carbon black is required for manufacturing tires that rail-

Acres of land filled with just used tires.

road cars transport it, and huge silos store the carbon black at the tire factory until it is needed.

Sulfur and other chemicals are also used in tires. Specific chemicals, when mixed with rubber and then heated, produce tire characteristics such as high friction (but low mileage) for a racing tire or high mileage (but lower friction) for a passenger car tire. Some chemicals keep the rubber flexible while it is being shaped into a tire while other chemicals protect the rubber from the ultraviolet radiation in sunlight.

## Tire Design

The main features of a passenger car tire are the tread, the body with sidewalls, and the beads. The tread is the raised pattern that comes in contact with the road. The body supports the tread and gives the tire its shape. The beads are rubber-covered, metal-wire bundles that hold the tire on the wheel.

Computer systems now play a major role in tire design. Complex analysis software based on years of test data allows tire engineers to simulate (imitate) the tread performance and durability of other designs. The software creates a three-dimensional color image of a possible tire design and calculates the effects of different stresses on the proposed design. Computer simulations save money for tire manufacturers because many design limitations can be discovered before a prototype (model or experimental) tire is actually assembled and tested.

In addition to tests of tread design and tire body construction, computers can simulate the effects of different types of rubber compounds. In a modern passenger car tire, as many as twenty different types of rubber may be used in different parts of the tire. One rubber compound may be used in the tread for good traction in cold weather; another compound is used to make sidewalls more rigid.

After tire engineers are satisfied with computer studies of a new tire, manufacturing engineers and skilled tire assemblers work with the designers to produce tire prototypes for testing. When design and manufacturing engineers are satisfied with a new tire design, tire factories begin mass production of the new tire.

## The Manufacturing Process

A passenger car tire is manufactured by wrapping multiple layers of specially formulated rubber around a metal drum in a tire-forming machine. The different parts of the tire are carried to the forming machine, where a skilled assembler cuts and positions the strips to form what is called the "green tire." When a green tire is finished, the metal drum collapses, allowing the tire assembler to remove the tire. The green tire is then taken to a mold for curing (finishing).

## Mixing the rubber

1 The first step in the tire manufacturing process is the mixing of raw materials to form the rubber compound (see fig. 54). Rail cars deliver large quantities of natural and synthetic rubber, carbon black, sulfur, and other chemicals and oils, all of which are stored until needed. Computer control systems contain various recipes and can automatically measure out specific batches of rubber and chemicals for mixing. Gigantic mixers, hanging like vertical cement mixers, stir the rubber and chemicals together in batches weighing up to 1,100 pounds.

**2** Each mix is then re-milled with additional heating to soften the batch and mix the chemicals. In a third step, the batch again goes through a mixer where additional chemicals are added to form what is known as the final mix. During all three steps of mixing, heat and friction are applied to soften the rubber and evenly distribute the chemicals. The chemical make up of each batch depends on the tire part—certain rubber formulas are used for the body, other formulas for the beads, and others for the tread.

## Body, beads, and tread

**3** Once a batch of rubber has been mixed, it goes through powerful rolling mills that press the batch into thick sheets. These sheets are then used to make the specific parts of the tire. The tire body, for instance, consists of strips of cloth-like fabric that are covered with rubber. Each strip of rubberized fabric is used to form a layer called a ply in the tire body. A passenger car tire may have as many as four plies in the body.

**4** For the beads of a tire, wire bundles are formed on a wire-wrapping machine. The bundles are then formed into rings, and the rings are covered with rubber.

**5** The rubber for the tire tread and sidewalls travels from the batch mixer to another type of processing machine called an extruder. In the extruder, the batch is further mixed and heated and then forced out through a die—a shaped opening—to form a layer of rubber. Sidewall rubber is covered with a protective plastic sheet, and rolled. Tread rubber is sliced into strips and loaded into large, flat metal cases called books (see fig. 54).

## Tire-building machine

**6** The rolls of sidewall rubber, the books containing tread rubber, and the racks of beads are all delivered to a skilled assembler at a tire-building machine (see fig. 54). At the center of the machine is a collapsible rotating drum that holds the tire parts. The tire assembler starts building a tire by wrapping the rubber-covered fabric plies of the body around the machine drum. After the ends of these plies are joined with glue, the beads are added and locked into place with additional body plies laid over the beads. Next, the assembler uses special power tools to shape the edges of the plies. Finally, the extruded rubber layers for the

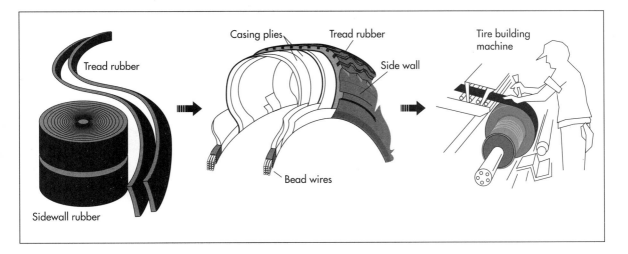

Fig. 54. The first step in the tire manufacturing process is the mixing of raw materials—rubber, carbon black, sulfur, and other materials—to form the rubber compound. After the rubber is prepared, it is sent to a tire-building machine, where a worker builds up the rubber layers to form the tire. At this point, the tire is called a "green tire."

sidewalls and tread are glued into place, and the assembled tire—the green tire—is removed from the tire-building machine (see fig. 55).

## Curing

7 A green tire is placed inside a large mold for the curing process (see fig. 55). A tire mold is shaped like a monstrous metal clam which opens to reveal a large, flexible balloon called a bladder. The green tire is placed over the bladder and, as the clamshell mold closes, the bladder fills with steam and expands to shape the tire and force the blank tread rubber against the raised interior of the mold. During this curing process, the steam heats the green tire up to 280 degrees Fahrenheit. Time in the mold depends on the characteristics desired in the tire.

8 After curing is complete, the tire is removed from the mold for cooling and testing. Each tire is thoroughly inspected for flaws such as bubbles or hollow spots in the rubber of the tread, sidewall, and interior of the tire. Then, the tire is placed on a test wheel, inflated, and spun. Sensors in the test wheel measure the balance of the tire and determine if it runs in a straight line. Once the tire has been inspected and run on the test wheel, it is moved to a warehouse for distribution.

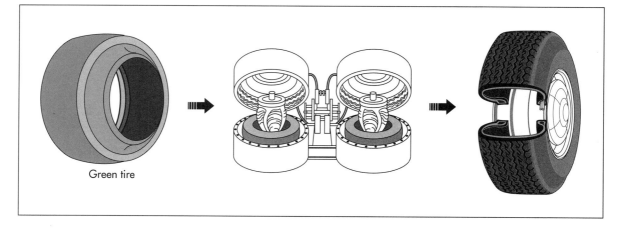

Fig. 55. After the green tire is made, it is put in a mold for curing. Shaped like a clam, the mold contains a large, flexible balloon. The tire is placed over the balloon (bladder), and the mold closes. Next, steam is pumped into the balloon, expanding it to shape the tire against the sides of the mold. After cooling, the tire is inflated and tested.

## Quality Control

Quality control begins with the suppliers of the raw materials. Tire manufacturers look for suppliers who test the raw materials before they are delivered to the tire plant. A manufacturer will often enter into special purchasing agreements with suppliers who provide detailed certification of the properties and make up of the raw materials. To insure the certification of suppliers, tire company chemists make random tests of the raw materials as they are delivered.

Throughout the batch-mixing process, samples of the rubber are drawn and tested to confirm different properties such as tensile strength (resistance to a tearing force) and density. Each tire assembler is responsible for the tire parts used. Code numbers and a comprehensive computer record-keeping system allow plant managers to trace batches of rubber and specific tire components.

When a new tire design is being manufactured for the first time, hundreds of tires are taken from the end of the assembly line for destructive testing. Some of the tires are sliced open to check for air pockets between body plies, while others are pressed down on metal studs to determine puncture resistance. Still other tires are spun rapidly and forced down onto metal drums to test mileage and other performance characteristics.

A variety of nondestructive evaluation techniques are also used in tire quality control. X-ray videography provides a quick and revealing view through a tire. In an X-ray test, a tire is selected at random and taken to a radiation booth where it is bombarded with X-rays. A technician views the image on a video screen, where tire defects are easily spotted. If a defect shows up, manufacturing engineers review the specific steps of tire component assembly to determine how the flaw was formed.

In addition to internal testing, feedback from consumers and tire dealers is also considered in the manufacturing process to determine what improvements are needed.

## Future Tires

Constant improvements in rubber chemistry and tire design are creating exciting new tires that offer greater mileage and improved performance in extreme weather conditions. Manufacturers now offer tires estimated to last up to 80,000 miles. Treads, designed and tested by computer, feature unique asymmetrical bands for improved traction and safety on wet or snowy roads.

Fun ways to recycle old tires.

Flat tires are so deflating. But there's some good news from tire design engineers. They've nearly perfected a non-pneumatic tire that will never go flat because it contains no pressurized air. One such non-pneumatic tire is simply one slab of thick plastic attached to the wheel rim. The plastic curves out from the rim to a point where a rubber tread is secured to the plastic for contact with the road. Such a tire offers lower rolling resistance for greater fuel economy and superior handling because of a greater area of contact between tread and road.

Another innovation is "run-flat" tire technology. These tires are able to withstand complete loss of air pressure, and still keep rolling smoothly for up to 200 miles. Manufacturers accomplish this by lining the inside with a special sealant which self-repairs punctures, and also by bolstering tire strength with extra tough sidewalls.

Tire production and experimentation just keeps rolling along, and will continue to improve as long as drivers demand it.

## WHERE TO LEARN MORE

Jacobs, Ed. "Black Art," *Popular Mechanics.* February 1993, pp. 29-31+.

Kovac, F.J. *Tire Technology.* Goodyear Tire and Rubber Co., 1978.

Lewington, Anna. *Antonio's Rainforest.* Carolrhoda Books, 1993.

Shepherd, Paul. "Wheels," *Omni.* January 1993, p. 11.

# *Trumpet*

## Brass Beginnings

A trumpet is a brass wind instrument noted for its powerful tone created by lip vibration against its cup-shaped mouthpiece. A trumpet consists of a cylindrical tube, shaped in an oblong loop that flares into a bell shape. Modern trumpets have three piston valves (for changing pitch) as well as small, secondary tubing that act as tuning slides to adjust the tone. Almost all trumpets played today are B-flat on the musical scale. This is the tone naturally sounded when the trumpet is blown. They have a range between the F-sharp below middle C to two and a half octaves above (ending at B), and are easier to play than most other brass instruments.

The first trumpets were most likely sticks that had been hollowed out by insects. Many early cultures, such as those in Africa and Australia, developed hollow, straight tubes for use as megaphones in religious rites. These early "trumpets" were made from cane, or from the horns or tusks of animals.

By 1400 B.C. the Egyptians had developed trumpets made from bronze and silver, with a wide bell. People in India, China, and Tibet also created trumpets, which were usually long and telescoped. Some, like Alpine horns, rested their bells on the ground.

Early European and Asian societies of Assyrians, Israelites, Greeks, Etruscans, Romans, Celts, and Teutonic tribes all had some form of horn, and many were decorated. These instruments, which produced low, powerful notes, were mainly used in battle or during ceremonies. They were not usually considered to be musical instruments.

*Ancient civilizations used the low, powerful notes of horns or trumpets as a call to battle, community assembly, or special ceremony. The musical potential of the horn was not explored until medieval times.*

A trumpet is a brass wind instrument noted for its powerful tone created by lip vibration against its cup-shaped mouthpiece.

To make these trumpets, the lost-wax method was used. With this process, wax was placed in a trumpet-shaped cavity (hollow area or hole). This mold was then heated, causing the wax to melt away, and in its place molten (melted) bronze was poured, producing a thick-walled instrument.

During the Crusades of the late Middle Ages (A.D. 1095-1270), Europeans were introduced to Arabic cultures. It is believed that trumpas, made from hammered sheets of metal, were first seen at this time. To make the tube of the trumpet, a sheet of metal was wrapped around a pole and soldered (joined or cemented with melted metal). To make the bell, a curved piece of metal, shaped somewhat like the arc of a phonograph record, was dovetailed (fit together exactly). One side was cut to form teeth which were alternately notched, then the other side of the piece was brought around and fastened between the teeth. The seam was smoothed out by hammering.

Around 1400 B.C. the long, straight trumpets were bent to make the same sound in a smaller, more convenient instrument. Molten lead was poured into the tube and allowed to solidify before it was beaten into a nearly perfect curve. The tube was then heated and the lead poured out. The first bent trumpets were S-shaped, but the form soon evolved into a more convenient oblong loop.

During the last half of the eighteenth century, as both musicians and trumpet makers searched for ways to make the instrument more versatile, a variety of trumpets were developed. One limitation of the trumpet of the 1700s was that it could not be played chromatically; that is, it could not play the half-step range called the chromatic scale. In 1750 Anton Joseph Hampel of Dresden suggested placing the hand in the bell to solve

Trumpeter Wynton Marsalis.

the problem. Around 1777 Michael Woggel and Johann Andreas Stein bent the trumpet to make it easier for the player's hand to reach the bell. But players found that this created more problems than it solved.

The keyed trumpet followed, but it never caught on, and was replaced by valve trumpets. The English created a slide trumpet, but many musicians found the slide difficult to control.

The first attempt to invent a valve mechanism was made by Charles Clagget, who took out a patent (government recognition of ownership of an invention) in 1788. The first practical device, however, was the box tubular valve invented by Heinrich Stoelzel and Friedreich Bluhmel in 1818. Joseph Riedlin in 1832 invented the rotary valve, a form now used only in Eastern Europe.

In 1839 Francois Perinet improved upon the tubular valve by inventing the piston-valved trumpet—the most preferred trumpet of today. Perinet's valves ensured a trumpet that was fully chromatic by effectively changing the length of the tube. An open valve lets air flow completely

During the U.S. Civil War (1861-1865), brass instruments gained enormous popularity. Every military unit had its own marching band. When peace was declared, the musicians were reluctant to "disband." They marched home and organized community brass bands in towns and cities across the country. Sunday concerts in neighborhood parks became a weekly event.

*Custom-made trumpets are highly personal instruments. The professional player will usually have his or her own favorite mouthpiece for which the custom-made trumpet is designed to accept.*

through the tube, while a closed valve diverts the air through its short, extra tubing before returning it to the main tube, lengthening its path. A combination of three valves provides all the variation a chromatic trumpet needs.

In 1842 the first trumpet factory was founded in Paris by Adolphe Sax. It was quickly imitated by large-scale manufacturers in England and the United States. Standardized parts, developed by Gustave Auguste Besson, became available in 1856. In 1875 C. G. Conn founded a factory in Elkhart, Indiana, and to this day most brass instruments from the United States are manufactured in Elkhart.

After so much musical progress, some musicians are now returning to former trumpet models. Many of today's orchestras find the B-flat trumpets too confining. There has been a revival of natural trumpets, rotary trumpets, and trumpets that produce a higher sound than the standard B-flat. Overall, however, modern trumpets produce high, brilliant, chromatic musical tones in contrast with the low, powerful, inaccurate instruments of the past.

## Trumpet Materials

Brass instruments are almost always made from brass, but solid gold or silver trumpets are sometimes created for special occasions. The most common type of brass used is yellow brass, which is 70 percent copper and 30 percent zinc. Other types include gold brass (80 percent copper and 20 percent zinc), and silver brass (made from copper, zinc, and nickel). The relatively small amount of zinc present in the alloy is necessary to make the brass workable when cold. Some small manufacturers use special brasses such as Ambronze (85 percent copper, 2 percent tin, and 13 percent zinc) for making certain parts of the trumpet (such as the bell). These alloys (metal mixtures) produce a richer, deeper, ringing sound when struck. Some manufacturers silver- or gold-plate the basic brass instrument, that is, coat it with a thin layer of the more-precious metal.

Though most of the trumpet is made of brass, screws are usually made of steel; the water key is generally lined with cork; the rubbing surfaces in the valves and slides is often electroplated (electrically coated with a thin layer) with chromium or a stainless nickel alloy such as monel.

The valves may be lined with felt; and the valve keys can be inlaid with mother-of-pearl.

## Trumpet Design

A good number of trumpets are intended for beginning students and are mass produced to provide reasonably priced, fairly high quality instruments. Mass-production creates replicas (copies) of excellent trumpets that are as exact as possible. Professional trumpeters, on the other hand, demand a higher priced, superior instrument, while trumpets for special events are almost always decorated, or engraved with ornate designs.

To meet the demand for custom-made trumpets, the manufacturer must determine the style of music that will be played, the type of orchestra or musical group that will be using the trumpet, and the desired quality of sound. The manufacturer can then provide a unique bell, specific shapes of the tuning slides, or different alloys or plating. Once the trumpet is created, the musician plays it to determine if any adjustments need to be made.

## The Manufacturing Process

### The main tube

1 The main tube of the trumpet is manufactured from standard machinable brass that is first put on a pole-shaped, tapered mandrel and lubricated (oiled to reduce friction) (see fig. 56). A die that looks like a doughnut is then drawn down its entire length, tapering and shaping it properly. Next, the shaped tube is annealed—heated (to around 1,000 degrees Fahrenheit or 538 degrees Celsius) to make it workable. This causes an oxide (oxygen compound) to form on the surface of the brass. To remove the oxidation, the tube is bathed in diluted sulfuric acid (a highly corrosive, oily liquid) before being bent.

2 The main tube may be bent using one of three different methods. Some manufacturers use hydraulic systems to push high pressure water through slightly bent tubing that has been placed in a die. The water presses the sides of the tubing to fit the mold exactly.

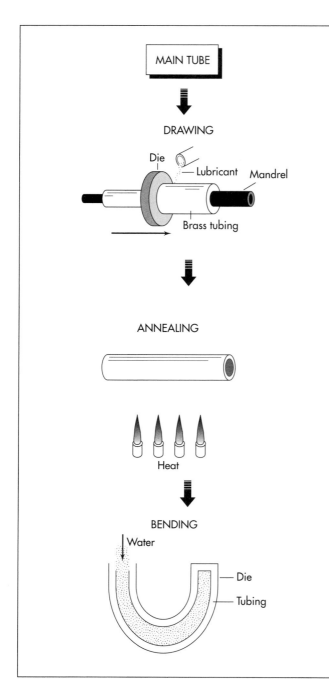

Fig. 56. The various parts of a trumpet are manufactured by drawing, hammering, bending, and annealing procedures.

Other manufacturers send ball bearings (hard metal balls) through the tubing. Smaller manufacturers pour pitch (a thick, dark, sticky substance) into the tube, let it cool, then use a lever to bend the tube into a standard curve before hammering it into shape.

## The bell

3 The bell is cut from sheet brass using an exact pattern. The flat, dress-shaped sheet is then hammered around a pole. Where the tube is cylindrical, the ends are brought together into a butt joint (end to end). Where the tube begins to flare, the ends are overlapped to form a lap joint. The entire joint is then brazed (soldered) with a propane oxygen flame at 1,500 to 1,600 degrees Fahrenheit (816 to 871 degrees Celsius) to seal it.

To make a rough bell shape, one end is hammered around the horn of a blacksmith anvil (a heavy block of metal on which other metals are shaped). The entire tube is then drawn on a mandrel exactly like the main tube, while the bell is spun on the mandrel. A thin wire is placed around the bell's rim, and metal is crimped (pinched or stamped) around it to give the edge its crisp appearance. The bell is then soldered to the main tube.

## The valves

4 The knuckles and extra tubing are first drawn on a mandrel as were the tube and bell. The knuckles are bent into 30-, 45-, 60-, and 90- degree

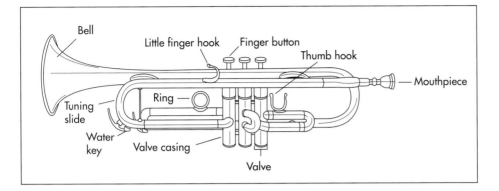

Fig. 57. Trumpets are almost always made of brass, but a solid gold or silver trumpet can be created for special occasions. The most common type of brass used is yellow brass, which is 70 percent copper and 30 percent zinc.

angles, and the smaller tubes are bent (using either the hydraulic or ball bearing methods used to bend the main tubing), annealed, and washed in acid to remove oxides and flux (substances added to ease the flow of soldering).

The valve cases are cut to length from heavy tubing and threaded at the ends. Holes are cut to match those of the pistons. Today, even small manufacturers use computer programs that precisely measure where the holes should be drawn. The valve cases can be cut with drills, using either pinpoint or rotary saw bits to cut the holes, after which pins prick out the scrap disk of metal. The knuckles, tubes, and valve cases are then placed in jigs (clamping devices) and their joints are painted with a solder and flux mixture using a blow torch.

After an acid bath, the assembly is polished on a buffing machine, using wax of varying grittiness, and muslin (coarse cloth) discs of varying roughness that rotate at high speeds (2,500 RPM [revolutions per minute] is typical).

## Assembly

5 The entire trumpet is now ready to be assembled. The side tubes for the valve slides are joined to the knuckles, and the main tubing is united end to end by overlapping the ferrules (metal ring placed around a pole or shaft to secure a joint) and soldering. Next, the pistons are inserted, the entire valve assembly is screwed onto the main tubing, and the mouthpiece is inserted.

**6** The trumpet is cleaned, polished, and lacquered (coated with a glossy finish), or it is sent to be electroplated. The finishing touch is to engrave the name of the company on a prominent piece of tubing. The lettering is transferred to the metal with carbon paper, and a skilled engraver carves the metal to match the etching.

**7** Trumpets are shipped either separately for special orders or in mass quantities for high school bands. They are wrapped carefully in thick plastic bubble packaging or other insulating material, placed in heavy boxes full of insulation (such as packaging peanuts) then mailed or sent by truck or rail to the customer.

## Quality Control

The most important feature of a trumpet is sound quality. Besides meeting exacting tolerances (permissible deviation from the standard) of approximately $1 \times 10^{-5}$ meters, every trumpet manufactured is tested by professional musicians who check the tone and pitch of the instrument while listening to see if it is within the desired dynamic, tuning range. The musicians test-play in different acoustical (listening) set-ups, ranging from small studios to large concert halls, depending on the eventual use of the trumpet. Large trumpet manufacturers employ professional musicians as full-time testers, while small manufacturers rely on themselves or the customer to test their product.

## The Owner's Responsibility

At least half the work involved in creating and maintaining a clear-sounding trumpet is done by the customer. The delicate instruments require special handling. Because of their precision and lack of symmetry, they are prone to imbalance, so great care must be taken to avoid damaging the instrument. To prevent dents, trumpets are kept in cases, where they are held in place by trumpet-shaped cavities that are lined with velvet.

Trumpets need to be lubricated once a day or each time they are played. The lubricant is usually a type of petroleum similar to kerosene for inside the valves, mineral oil for the key mechanism, and axle grease for the slides. The mouthpiece and main pipe should be cleaned every month, and every three months the entire trumpet should be soaked in soapy water for 15 minutes. It should then be scrubbed with special small brushes, rinsed, and dried.

A trumpet player in a marching band.

To maintain the life of a trumpet, it must occasionally undergo repairs. Large dents can be removed by annealing and hammering; small dents can be hammered out and balls passed through to test the final size; cracks can be patched; and worn pistons can be replated and ground back to their former size.

After all the cleaning chores are complete, the step left is to practice, practice, and practice!

## WHERE TO LEARN MORE

Ardley, Neil. *Eyewitness Books: Music.* Alfred A. Knopf, 1989.

Ardley, Neil. *Music: An Illustrated Encyclopedia.* Facts on File, 1986.

Barclay, Robert. *The Art of the Trumpet-Maker.* Oxford University Press, 1992.

Macaulay, David. *The Way Things Work.* Houghton Mifflin Company, 1988.

Weaver, James C. "The Trumpet Museum," *Antiques and Collecting Hobbies.* January 1990, pp. 30-33+.

# Watch

*Mechanical timepieces are complex inventions filled with wheels, gears, levers, and springs. Digital watches keep people on schedule with quartz crystals, circuit boards, and microchips.*

## Tracking Time

The White Rabbit from *Alice's Adventures in Wonderland* probably said it best. "I'm late, I'm late, for a very important date." Humans have worried and struggled to be on time for work and play since time began. They've watched the sun and listened to roosters, relied on shadows cast by sundials and on sand sifting through an hourglass. The invention of an accurate wristwatch leaves humanity without an excuse for being tardy.

The oldest means of determining time is by observing the location of the sun in the sky. When the sun is directly overhead, the time is roughly 12:00 noon. A slightly later development, and one less dependent on an individual's judgment, is the use of a sundial. During the daylight hours, sunlight falls on a vertical pole placed at the center of a standard dial, thus casting a shadow on the dial and producing a relatively accurate time reading.

The invention of the mechanical clock in the fourteenth century was a major advancement—it was a smaller and more consistent method of measuring time. The mechanical clock includes a complicated series of wheels, gears, and levers powered by falling weights and a pendulum (or later a wound-up spring). Together these pieces moved the hand or hands on a dial to show the time. The addition of chimes or gongs on the hour, half hour, and quarter hour followed soon afterward. By the eighteenth century, smaller clocks which were enclosed or sealed for home use became available.

The more exacting the workmanship of the moving parts, the more accurate the clock. From its invention through to the middle of the twentieth century, developments in clock-making focused on making the moving parts work as accurately as possible. Horological science (time measurement) required improvements of several important materials and skills. Developments were needed in metal technology, in miniaturization, and the lubrication of small parts. Craftsman needed the skills to use natural sapphires (and later artificial sapphires) at the spots that received the most stress (the jeweled movement).

Small pocket watches, perhaps two to three inches (five to seven centimeters) in diameter, were available by the end of the nineteenth century. Mechanical wristwatches were an everyday item in the United States by the 1960s. But the central problem faced by watch and clockmakers remained the same: mechanical parts wore down, became inaccurate, and broke.

During the daylight hours, sunlight falls on a vertical pole placed at the center of a standard dial, thus casting a shadow on the dial and producing a relatively accurate time reading.

In the years immediately following World War II, interest in atomic physics led to the development of the atomic clock. Radioactive materials emit (send out) particles at a known, steady rate. The meshing gears and parts of a mechanical clock that keep time could be replaced by a device that imitated the watch movement each time a particle was emitted by the radioactive element. Atomic clocks, incidentally, are still made and sold, and are consistently accurate.

*At one time watches were expensive devices for royalty or the very rich.*

## The Quartz Watch

With the development of the microchip in the 1970s and 1980s, a new type of watch was invented. Wristwatches that mixed microchip technology with quartz crystals became the standard; there are few non-quartz wristwatches made today. The microchip is used to send continuous sig-

*Horology is the very precise science of measuring time or making clocks and watches.*

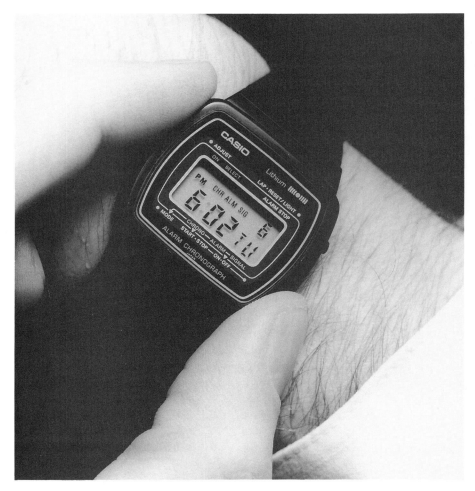

A man wearing a digital watch.

nals to the dial of the watch. Because it is not a mechanical device with moving parts, it never wears out.

The use of quartz in watches takes advantage of a long-known type of electricity known as piezoelectricity. Piezoelectricity is the current which flows from or through a piece of quartz when the quartz is put under electrical and/or mechanical pressure (piezo is from the Greek verb meaning "to press"). A quartz watch uses the electricity from a piece of quartz subjected to the electricity from a battery to send a regular, countable series of signals (oscillations or vibrations) to one or more microchips.

The most accurate quartz watches are those in which the time appears in an electronically controlled digital display, produced by a light-emitting diode (LED) or a liquid crystal display (LCD). It is possible to have the microprocessor (central processing part) send its signals to mechanical devices that make hands move on the watch face, creating an analog display. But because the hands are mechanically operated through a part of the watch called the gear train, analog watches usually are not as accurate or long-wearing as digitals. Both types of watches achieve tremendous accuracy, with digital watches commonly being accurate to within three seconds per month.

## Watch Materials

Electronic watches make use of many of the most modern materials available, including plastics and alloy metals (mixtures of two or more metals). Cases can be made of either plastic or metal; watches with metal cases often include a stainless steel backing.

Microchips are typically made of silicon (a nonmetallic crystalline element), while LEDs are usually made of gallium arsenide, gallium phosphide, or gallium arsenide phosphide (all semiconductors). LCDs consist of liquid crystals sandwiched between glass pieces. Electrical contacts between parts are usually made of a small amount of gold (or gold-plating), which is an almost ideal electrical conductor and can be used successfully in very small amounts.

## The Manufacturing Process

This section will focus on quartz digital watches with LED displays. Although the assembly of such watches must be careful and methodical, the most important steps of the production process are in the manufacture of the separate parts.

### Quartz

1 The heart of a quartz watch is a tiny sliver of quartz. The synthetically produced (man-made) quartz is cut by the manufacturer with a diamond saw (special tool for cutting extremely hard materials) and shipped to the watchmaker. The production of "grown" quartz is a critical step in the process.

Quartz, in its natural form, is first loaded into a giant kettle or autoclave (the same device used by doctors and dentists to sterilize instruments) (see fig. 58). Hanging from the top of the autoclave are seeds or tiny

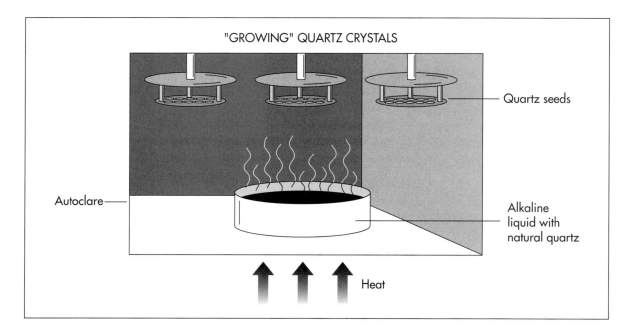

"GROWING" QUARTZ CRYSTALS

Quartz seeds

Autoclare

Alkaline liquid with natural quartz

Heat

Fig. 58. In a natural form, quartz is first loaded into a giant kettle or autoclave. Hanging from the top of the autoclave are seeds or tiny particles of quartz with the desired crystalline structure. An alkaline material is pumped into the bottom of the autoclave, and heated to a high temperature which dissolves the quartz in the hot alkaline liquid, evaporates it, and deposits it onto the seeds.

particles of quartz with the desired crystalline structure. An alkaline material is pumped into the bottom of the autoclave, and the autoclave is heated to a temperature of around 750 degrees Fahrenheit (400 degrees Celsius). The natural quartz dissolves in the hot alkaline liquid, evaporates, and deposits itself onto the seeds. As it deposits itself, it follows the pattern of the crystalline structure of the seeds. After about 75 days, the chamber can be opened, and the newly grown quartz crystals can be removed and cut into the correct proportions. Different angles and thicknesses in the cutting enhance the predictable rates of oscillation (to swing back and forth between two points—similar to a pendulum). The desired rate of oscillation for quartz used in wristwatches is 100,000 megaHertz or 100,000 oscillations per second. Eventually the oscillation rate will be reduced significantly and then interpreted into seconds by microchips (see step 4).

2 To work most effectively, the piece of quartz needs to be sealed in a vacuum chamber of one sort or another. Most commonly, the quartz is placed into a sort of capsule, with wires attached to both ends,

allowing the capsule to be soldered or otherwise connected to a circuit board.

## The microchip

3 The electronic leads generated by a battery through the quartz (producing oscillations) will go to a microchip that serves as a "frequency dividing circuit" (see fig. 59). Microchip manufacture, like the quartz, is also carried out by the supplier to the watch manufacturer. An extensive and complex process, making microchips involves chemical and/or x-ray etching of a microscopic electronic circuit (to conduct the current) onto a tiny piece of silicon dioxide.

4 The oscillation rate of perhaps 100,000 vibrations per second is reduced to 1 or 60 or some other more manageable number of oscillations. The new pattern of oscillation is then sent to another microchip that functions as a "counter-decoder-driver." This chip will actually count the oscillations that it receives. If there are sixty oscillations per second, the chip will change the reading on an LED every second. After 3,600 oscillations (60 x 60), the counter will instruct the LED to change the reading for minutes. And, after 60 x 60 x 60 oscillations (216,000), the counter will change the hour reading.

## Assembly

5 The entire set of crystal and microchips is set onto a circuit board (see fig. 59) The board has a space

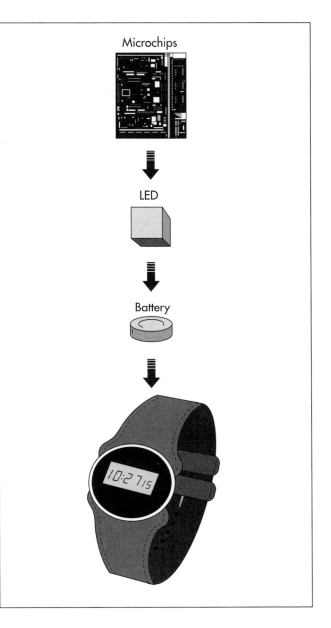

Fig. 59. In watch assembly, the entire set of crystal and microchips is set onto a circuit board. A battery is also installed which generates electricity for the quartz crystal and supplies the power to the LED display.

to hold the battery that supplies electricity to the quartz crystal. This battery powers the LED display. Generally, the space for the battery is on the outside of the surface facing the back of the case. This way the battery can be replaced by removing the back of the watch, shaking out the old one, and dropping in the new battery.

6 The mechanism used for setting the watch is then connected. This mechanism involves two pins that extend beyond the case of the watch. One pin lets the counter circuit know which reading to reset—seconds, minutes, or hours. The second pin is pushed a number of times to bring the display to the desired reading.

7 The entire circuit board, along with a battery, is then closed into a case, and a wrist strap is attached.

## Extra Watch-Works

High-tech wristwatches do much more than just tell time. Microchips in a quartz watch are capable of holding large quantities of information in a very small space. Therefore it is possible for engineers to add other functions to a watch without much difficulty. An extra push button on the case connected to the internal counter circuit can provide plenty of fancy time tricks for the demanding customer.

Countdown timers, alarms, and water-resistance are a few features available. Some sports watches can provide altitude and depth measurements, tide information, a compass for direction, and a speed measurement device. The microchip can be easily programmed to set the watch forward or back at the push of a button, so jetsetters can determine the time in different time zones, or perhaps have two, three, or more time zone times displayed successively.

## Quality Control

All components of electronic watches are manufactured under a strict system of quality control. Quartz crystals, for example, have their frequencies tested before being used in a watch. Microchips must be made in a "clean room" environment with specially filtered air, since even the tiniest dust particles can ruin them. Microchips are examined carefully and tested for accuracy before use.

After a watch is manufactured, it is tested again before being shipped to market. In addition to its time-keeping accuracy, it is also subjected to a drop-test in which it must continue to operate properly after being dropped and otherwise abused; a temperature test; and a water test. A watchmaker may, with proper testing and proof, claim that a watch is "water resistant" at certain depths. However it is inaccurate to say a watch is "waterproof" because without specific design and explanation of allowances, that claim is meaningless.

Large watch companies make all of their own parts, ensuring that product quality standards are in place at the earliest point in the manufacturing process.

## Future Time

Today's electronic watches are extremely accurate. Some watch makers claim their inventions are capable of keeping time with less than a one second variance in three million years.

This Casio watch features a face that flips up to a mini-computer to store names, numbers, and other data.

Future innovations in watch designing will take advantage of technologies from other fields. Look for such extras as the addition of a calculator or even a radio-transmitter that can send out a traceable signal if the wearer is lost or in trouble. There's no stopping the advances—and there's no stopping time.

## WHERE TO LEARN MORE

Aust, Siegfried. *Clocks! How Time Flies.* Lerner Publications, 1991.
Billings, Charlene W. *Microchip: Small Wonder.* Dodd Mead & Company, 1984.
*How Things Are Made.* National Geographic Society, 1981.
Macaulay, David. *The Way Things Work.* Houghton Mifflin Company, 1988.
*The Visual Dictionary of Everyday Things.* Dorling Kindersley, 1991.

# Zipper

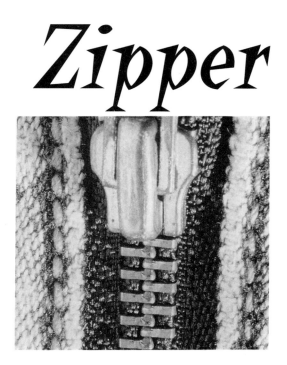

## Closure for Clothes

Keeping clothes closed is an engineering feat of modern times. Cavemen fastened their hides with bone or horn pins secured by bone splinters. We've come a long way from these early efforts to keep warm.

Many devices were designed later that were more efficient. Early fasteners included buckles, laces, safety pins, and buttons. Buttons with buttonholes, while still an important practical method of closure even today, had their difficulties. Zippers were first invented to replace the irritating nineteenth-century practice of buttoning up twenty to forty tiny buttons on each shoe.

In 1851, Elias Howe, the inventor of the sewing machine, developed what he called an automatic continuous clothing closure. It consisted of a series of clasps united by a connecting cord running or sliding upon ribs. Despite the potential of this ingenious breakthrough, the invention was never marketed.

Another inventor, Whitcomb L. Judson, came up with the idea of a slide fastener, which he patented (got government permission to control) in 1893. Judson's mechanism was an arrangement of hooks and eyes with a slide clasp that connected them. After Judson displayed the new clasp lockers at the 1893 World's Columbian Exposition in Chicago, he obtained financial backing from Lewis Walker, and together they founded the Universal Fastener Company in 1894.

The first zippers were not much of an improvement over buttons, and innovations came slowly over the next decade. Judson invented a zipper

*"Zippers" earned their name from the metallic hiss heard when a slider is pulled quickly up or down.*

that parted completely (like the zippers found on today's jackets), and discovered that it was better to clamp the teeth directly onto a cloth tape that could be sewn into a garment, rather than have the teeth themselves sewn onto the garment.

Zippers were still prone to popping open and sticking as late as 1906, when Otto Frederick Gideon Sundback joined Judson's company, then called the Automatic Hook and Eye Company. His patent for Plako in 1913 is considered to be the beginning of the modern zipper.

Sundback's "Hookless Number One," a device in which jaws clamped down on beads, was quickly replaced by "Hookless Number Two", which was very similar to modern zippers. Nested, cup-shaped teeth formed the best zipper to date, and a machine that could stamp out the metal in one process made marketing the new fastener possible.

A zipper on a jacket.

The first zippers were introduced for use in World War I as fasteners for soldiers' money belts, flying suits, and life-vests. Because of the war, many materials were in short supply for civilian use. Therefore, Sundback developed a new zipper machine that used only about 40 percent of the metal required by older machines.

Zippers for the general public were not produced until the 1920s, when B. F. Goodrich requested them for use in its company galoshes (overshoes or boots). It was Goodrich president, Bertram G. Work, who came up with the word zipper, but he meant it to refer to the boots themselves, and not the device that fastened them, which he felt was more properly called a slide fastener.

Zippers changed again during the 1940s as a result of World War II. Zipper factories in Germany had been destroyed, and metal was scarce. A West German company, Opti-Werk GmbH, began research into new plas-

*The first, hookless zippers were manufactured for use on corsets, gloves, money belts, sleeping bags, and tobacco pouches.*

tics, and this research resulted in numerous patents. J. R. Ruhrman and his associates were granted a German patent for developing a plastic ladder chain. In 1940 Alden W. Hanson devised a method that allowed a plastic coil to be sewn into the zipper's cloth. This was followed by a notched plastic wire, developed independently by A. Gerbach and the firm William Prym-Wencie, that could actually be woven into the cloth.

After a slow start, zipper sales began to soar. In 1917 24,000 zippers were sold; in 1934 the number had risen to 60 million. Today zippers are easily produced and sold by the billions, for everything from blue jeans to sleeping bags.

## Zipper Materials

The basic elements of a zipper are:

- the stringer (the tape and teeth assembly that makes up one side of a zipper);
- the slider (opens and closes the zipper);
- a tab (pulled to move the slider); and stops (prevent the slider from leaving the chain).

Instead of a bottom stop to connect the stringers, a separating zipper has two devices—a box and a pin—that work as stops when put together (see fig. 60).

Metal zipper hardware can be made of stainless steel, aluminum, brass, zinc, or a nickel-silver alloy (metal mixture). Sometimes a steel zipper will be coated with brass or zinc, or painted to match the color of the cloth tape or garment.

Zippers with plastic hardware are made from polyester or nylon, while the slider and pull tab are usually made from steel or zinc. The cloth tapes are either made from cotton, polyester, or a blend of both. For zippers that open on both ends (as in a jacket), the ends are not usually sewn into a garment, so that they are hidden as they are when a zipper is made to open at only one end. These zippers are strengthened using a strong cotton tape (that has been reinforced with nylon) applied to the ends to keep the cloth from fraying.

## The Manufacturing Process

Today's zippers have key components of either metal or plastic. Beyond this one very important difference, the steps involved in producing the finished product are basically the same.

## Making stringers—metal zippers

**1** A stringer consists of the tape (or cloth) and teeth that make up one side of the zipper (see fig. 60). Early production methods were slow and tedious. Faster manufacturing methods, originating in the 1940s, involved a flattened strip of wire passing between a heading punch and a pocket punch to form scoops. A blanking punch cuts around the scoops to form a Y shape. The legs of the Y are then clamped around the cloth tape.

**2** Yet another method, developed in the 1930s, uses molten metal to form teeth. A mold, shaped like a chain of teeth, is clamped around the cloth tape. Molten zinc under pressure is then injected into the mold. Water cools the mold, which then releases the shaped teeth. Any left-over metal is trimmed off.

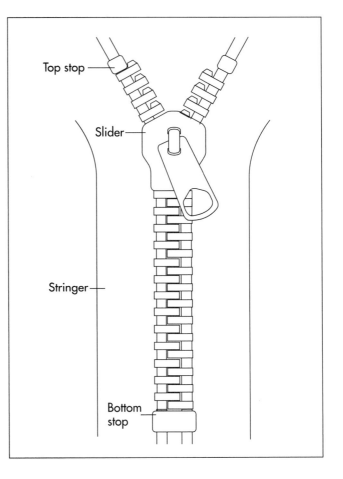

Fig. 60. The basic elements of a zipper.

## Making stringers—plastic zippers

**3** Plastic zippers can be spiral, toothed, ladder, or woven directly into the fabric. Two methods are used to make the stringers for a spiral plastic zipper. The first involves notching a round plastic wire before feeding it between two heated screws. These screws, one rotating clockwise, the other counterclockwise, pull the plastic wire out to form loops. A head maker at the front of each loop then forms it into a round knob. Next, the plastic spiral is cooled with air. This method requires that a left spiral and right spiral be made simultaneously (at the same time) on two separate machines so that the chains will match up on a finished zipper.

The second method for spiral plastic zippers makes both the left and right spiral simultaneously on one machine (see fig. 61). A piece of wire is

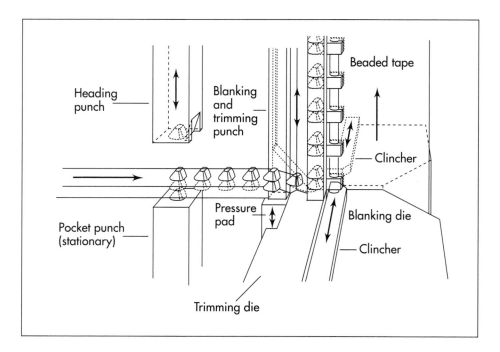

Fig. 61. A stringer consists of the tape (or cloth) and teeth that make up one side of the zipper. One method of making the stringer involves passing a flattened strip of wire between a heading punch and a pocket punch to form scoops. A blanking punch cuts around the scoops to form a Y shape. The legs of the Y are then clamped around the cloth tape.

looped twice between notches on a rotating forming wheel. A pusher and head maker simultaneously press the plastic wires firmly into the notches and form the heads. This process makes two chains that are already linked together to be sewn onto two cloth tapes.

4  To make the stringers for a toothed plastic zipper, a molding process is used that is similar to the metal process described in step 2. A rotating wheel has several small molds on its edge that are shaped like flattened teeth. Two cords run through the molds and connect the finished teeth. Semi-molten plastic is fed into the mold, where it is held until it solidifies. A folding machine bends the teeth into a U-shape that can be sewn onto a cloth tape.

5  The stringers for a ladder plastic zipper are made by winding a plastic wire onto alternating spools that protrude from the edge of a rotating forming wheel. Strippers on each side lift the loops off the

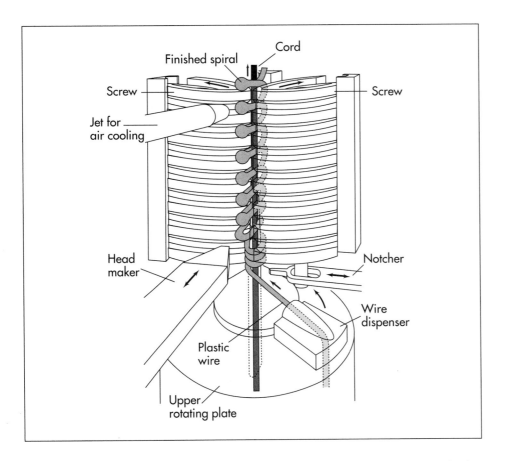

Fig. 62. To make the stringer for a spiral plastic zipper, a round plastic wire is notched and then fed between two heated screws. These screws, one rotating clockwise, the other counterclockwise, pull the plastic wire out to form loops. A head maker at the front of each loop then forms it into a round knob. This method requires that a left spiral and right spiral be made simultaneously (at the same time) on two separate machines so that the chains will match up on a finished zipper.

spools while a heading and notching wheel simultaneously press the loops into a U-shape and form heads on the teeth, which are then sewn onto the cloth tape.

6 Superior garment zippers can be made by weaving the plastic wire directly into the cloth, using the same method as is used in cloth weaving. This method is not common in the United States, but such zippers are frequently imported from other countries.

## Completing the manufacturing process

**7** Once the individual stringers have been made, they are joined together with a temporary device similar to a slider. They are then pressed, and, in the case of metal zippers, wire brushes scrub down sharp edges. The tapes are then starched (soaked in a stiffening solution), wrung out, and dried. Metal zippers are waxed for smooth operation, and both types are rolled onto huge spools to be formed later into complete zippers.

**8** After being stamped or die-cast (stamped or molded) from metal, the slider and pull tab are assembled separately. The continuous zipper tape is then unrolled from the spool and its teeth are removed at intervals, leaving spaces that surround smaller chains. For zippers that only open on one end, the bottom stop is clamped on, and the slider is threaded onto the chain. Next, the top stops are clamped on, and the gaps between lengths of teeth are cut at midpoint. For zippers that separate, the midpoint of each gap is coated with reinforcing tape, and the top stops are clamped on. The tape is then sliced to separate the strips of chain again. The slider and the box are then slipped onto one chain, and the pin is slipped onto the other.

**9** Finished zippers are stacked, placed in boxes, and trucked to clothing manufacturers, luggage manufacturers, or any of the other manufacturers that rely on zippers. Some are also shipped to department stores or fabric shops for direct purchase by the consumer.

## Quality Control

Zippers, despite their nearly worry-free use, are complicated devices that rely on the smooth, almost perfect linkage of tiny cupped teeth. Because they are usually designed as fasteners for clothing, they must pass a series of tests to ensure they can withstand frequent washing and the stress of everyday wear.

Every dimension of a zipper—its width, length, tape end lengths, teeth dimensions, length of chain, slide dimensions, and stop lengths—is subject to checking values that must fall within an acceptable range. Samplers use statistical analysis to check the range for a batch of zippers. Generally, the dimensions of the zipper must be within 90 percent of the desired length, though in most cases it is closer to 99 percent.

A zipper on a soft suitcase.

A zipper is tested for flatness and straightness. Flatness is measured by passing a gauge set at a certain height; if the gauge touches the zipper several times, that zipper is defective. To measure straightness, the zipper is laid across a straight edge and checked for any curving.

Zipper strength is very important. The teeth should not come off easily, nor should the zipper be easy to break. To test for strength, a tensile (tearing) testing machine is attached by a hook to a tooth. The machine then pulls, and a gauge measures the force at which the tooth separates from the cloth. These same tensile testing machines are used to determine the strength of the entire zipper. A machine is attached to each cloth tape, then pulled. The force required to pull the zipper completely apart into two separate pieces is measured. Acceptable strength values are determined according to what type of zipper is being made: a heavy-duty zipper will be stronger than a lightweight one. Zippers are also compressed (crushed) to establish their breaking point.

To measure a zipper for ease of closure, a tensile testing machine measures the force needed to zip it up and down. For clothing, this value should be quite low, so that the average person can zip with ease and so that the cloth does not tear. For other purposes, such as mattress covers, the force can be higher.

A finished sample zipper must meet textile quality controls. It is tested for laundering durability by being washed in a small amount of hot water, a significant amount of bleach and abrasives (rough materials) to imitate many washings. Zippers are also agitated with small steel balls to test the coating for abrasion.

The cloth of the tapes must be colorfast. For example, if the garment is to be dry cleaned only, its zipper must be colorfast during the dry cleaning process.

Shrinkage is also tested. Two marks are made on the cloth tape. After the zipper is heated or washed, the change in length between the two marks is measured. Heavyweight zippers should have no shrinkage. A lightweight zipper should have a one to four percent shrinkage rate.

All this testing and checking have paid off. Despite the continued use of buttons, bows, rivets, and snaps, zippers are still up front. Even the introduction and invasion of velcro closures haven't chased them off the market. Zippers are still popular for their flexible strength and reliability. They're hidden in seams for simple function or stitched in obvious spots for a colorful fashion statement. Today zippers are used in clothing, shoes, luggage, tents, almost anything made of cloth that needs to be opened and closed.

## WHERE TO LEARN MORE

Caney, Steven. *Invention Book.* Workman Publishing, 1985.
Macaulay, David. *The Way Things Work.* Houghton Mifflin Company, 1988.
Panati, Charles. *Extraordinary Origins of Everyday Things.* Harper & Row, 1987.
Petroskey, Henry. *The Evolution of Useful Things.* Alfred A. Knopf, 1992.
*Reader's Digest: How in the World?* Reader's Digest, 1990.
*Zipper! An Exploration in Novelty.* W.W. Norton & Co., 1994.

# Index

**Boldfacing**
indicates entrants

Bynema  49

# C

# D

Dutch cocoa  67
Dutched  69

# E

E-coat  8
E. I. du Pont de Nemours & Co.  48
Ebony  109
Edison, Thomas Alva  146
Electric automobile  11
Electric guitar  113
Electrodes  145
Electroforming  85
Electromagnetic induction  210
Electroplated  258, 262
Endoscope  173
Engraving  185, 242
Engraving method  185
Environmental Protection Agency
    (EPA)  242
Enzymes  68
EPA (see Environmental Protection
    Agency)
Epoxy  121
Etching  269
Ethylene vinyl acetate  194
Ewing, James Alfred  210
Extruder  250
**Eyeglass lens  89-97**

# F

Fahrenheit, Gabriel Daniel  239
Faraday, Michael  210
Father (CD manufacturing)  86
FDA (see Food and Drug
    Administration)
Ferdinand II  238
Fermentation  68
Ferrules  261
Fiberglass  48
Filament  126, 146
Filming  41
Flaming cabinet  160
Flashlights  149
Flat  41
**Floppy Disk  98-106**
Fluorescent lamps  147

Fluoride  173
Flux  261
Font  39
Food and Drug Administration (FDA)
    97
Ford, Henry  1-2
Forged  122
Formaldehyde  165
Freeblowing  124
Frets  107
Fuselage  120

# G

Galileo  238
Galley  39
Galoshes  273
Galvanometer  210
Gama, Vasco da  219
Gate  73
Generator  94
Genovese  27
Gerbach, A.  274
Germanium  14
Ginned cotton  30
Glass  84, 89
Glassblowing  241
Glue  229
Gold  83
Goldenrod  41
Golitsyn, Boris  210
Goodyear, Charles  191, 247
Gore  193
Granulator  227
Gravure  42, 185
Gray, Thomas  210
Greeks  46
Grinding  94
**Guitar  107-114**
Gutenberg, Johann  36

# H

Halftones  41
Halide  147
Hampel, Anton Joseph  256
Hanson, Alden W.  274
Harnesses  142